PRACTICAL PEDAGOGY FOR THE JEWISH CLASSROOM

Recent Titles in
The Greenwood Educators' Reference Collection

PRACTICAL PEDAGOGY FOR THE JEWISH CLASSROOM

Classroom Management, Instruction, and Curriculum Development

Daniel B. Kohn

The Greenwood Educators'
Reference Collection

GREENWOOD PRESS
Westport, Connecticut • London

Library of Congress Cataloging-in-Publication Data

Kohn, Daniel B., 1963–
    Practical pedagogy for the Jewish classroom : classroom
management, instruction, and curriculum development / Daniel B.
Kohn.
        p.   cm.—(The Greenwood educators' reference collection,
ISSN 1056–2192)
    Includes bibliographical references and index.
    ISBN 0–313–30931–0 (alk. paper)
    1. Jewish religious education of teenagers.   2. Jewish religious
education—Teaching methods.   I. Title.   II. Series.
BM108.K65   1999
296.6'8'0835—dc21   98–29676

British Library Cataloguing in Publication Data is available.

Library of Congress Catalog Card Number: 98–29676
ISBN: 0–313–30931–0
ISSN: 1056–2192

First published in 1999

Greenwood Press, 88 Post Road West, Westport, CT 06881
An imprint of Greenwood Publishing Group, Inc.

Printed in the United States of America

The paper used in this book complies with the
Permanent Paper Standard issued by the National
Information Standards Organization (Z39.48–1984).

10 9 8 7 6 5 4 3 2 1

This book is dedicated with love to:

My parents, who encouraged me to strive to achieve my goals no matter how seemingly distant;

and

My wife, Deborah, who is teaching me the most important lessons in life.

Contents

Acknowledgments

Many people influenced me and inspired me to write this book. I could not have done it if I had not worked at one of the most unique, exciting, and effective Jewish high schools in the country, the Solomon Schechter High School of Long Island (SSHSLI). As one of the first four full-time faculty members when the school was founded in the Fall of 1994, I am indebted to Mark Meiri, Miriam Fisher, and Leslie Bazer for some of the most stimulating and thought-provoking discussions in that first, tumultuous, electrifying year of the high school's existence. Special thanks to Mark Meiri for his wisdom, insight, and friendship. I am particularly grateful for his insistent encouragement to create the class, "Living on God's Earth" (see the section, "Teaching Morality," page 80). Also, I could not, nor would, have written this book if it had not been for the help, insight, and support of my friend and colleague Rabbi Jonathan Spira-Savett. His vision and approach to education was invaluable when and where mine failed.

To the entire, growing faculty of the SSHSLI, particularly the Judaic Studies department and Riki Weiderhorn, Shira Birk, Flora Yavelberg, and Judith May, I owe a debt of gratitude for the conversations and opportunities that enabled me to grow as a teacher. I am also indebted to all of the students whom I have taught—and who have taught me—in all of my classes. Through their questions and comments, I continued to learn more about subjects that I once thought I understood.

I am grateful to my parents for encouraging me to strive for excellence in all of my endeavors, especially my father, whose literary accomplishments inspired my own. Finally, I owe the most to my wife, Deborah Lee Stachel, for her love as a friend and spouse and for her profoundly gifted insights into education and my soul.

Introduction

"The other kids are horrible, the teacher is a fool, and it's a waste of time anyway because I don't learn anything." This is the typical response of many Jewish teenagers when it comes to describing their experiences in Hebrew school/Sunday school/Hebrew high school/Jewish day school. Students know best what the deficiencies of Jewish education are—classroom management, the caliber of the teachers, and the quality of curricula. Unless we address these issues, all of the money and effort currently being devoted to Jewish education will be wasted. How did we get into this situation?

In 1990, the National Jewish Population Survey ignited a debate in the American Jewish community about the survival and future of Jews in this country. The results, which were well publicized (as well as disputed), revealed tremendous assimilation, alienation, and intermarriage within the American Jewish community. These findings sparked a renewed interest in Jewish education in the United States. This commitment to Jewish continuity has been translated directly into support for Jewish education. Synagogues are spending more money on their informal and Hebrew high school programs, Jewish Federations are vastly increasing their efforts to boost teen tours of Israel, and many organization are working to improve the Jewish day school movement. Orthodox days schools are more popular than ever; and in addition to the Reform, Conservative, and communal full-time Jewish day schools that were already in existence, the number of new non-Orthodox Jewish schools, especially high schools, has been expanding throughout the country as a result of this new-found commitment to Jewish education.

Why has the Jewish community chosen to focus on Jewish education especially during the high school years? Many Jewish educators have begun to realize that the high school years are the time when young adults develop more sophisticated ways of perceiving and understanding the world around them. During the ages of approximately fourteen to eighteen, teenagers develop tremendously significant new capacities to absorb new information and modes of thinking and, perhaps more importantly, the desire and ability to forge a sense of their own individual and communal identity. Jewish education during the high school years—whether it comes in the form of a full-time Jewish day school, synagogue confirmation class, communal Jewish day school, or supplemental Hebrew high school—is the most propitious and effective time in which to try and instill in Jewish teenagers a love and passion for Jewish learning and living.

However, little effort has been expended on improving the *quality* of this education. Despite the interest in the field of teenage Jewish education, the investment of the Jewish community will be in vain unless it addresses the problems of classroom management, teacher training, and the development of quality Jewish Studies curricula. This book is dedicated to the discussion of these topics and providing suggestions for improvement.

Why did I write this book? When I first entered the world of Jewish education, I was surprised to discover how few books there were that even acknowledged these problems, let alone that were devoted to issues of practical pedagogy for the Jewish teacher. Many of the Jewish educational journals published today are aimed at administrators, particular organizations or institutions, or are written for an academic audience in education. While such journals are vitally important to the burgeoning field of Jewish pedagogy, I recognized that, despite my own extensive rabbinical education, I needed more materials that offered me *practical* advice and guidance about how to develop my own strategies for effective classroom management and how to grow as a teacher and Jewish educator, as well as educational material so that I could create my own, unique approach to teaching Jewish studies.

Who is this book intended for? I wrote this book for myself, my colleagues in the world of Jewish education, synagogue youth department leaders, rabbis, administrators, trustees and education board members, and parents. This book is for everyone associated with or even just interested in Jewish education. It is a handbook for students of education, beginning teachers, and veteran educators who have already accrued years of experience and expertise in their fields. It is a blueprint for administrators, principals, and board members involved in Jewish education. It is intended for everyone connected with Jewish education in every possible setting that affects Jewish teens and children. But, most importantly, it is a manifesto for the future of quality Jewish education for new generations of American Jews.

This book is divided into three parts that address the three major problem areas of Jewish education today. The first part deals with issues of classroom management as it relates to student behavior, teacher response, administrative policies, and involvement of parents. It addresses the question of what can a teacher do to influence and improve the learning environment in the classroom. The answers range from beginning and ending each Jewish Studies class with blessings over Torah study; developing interpersonal skills; striving to become a better, more even-tempered individual; recognizing the limits of the student–teacher relationship; giving tests; instituting a classroom discipline policy and following it up with negative consequences; as well as establishing and maintaining an ongoing dialogue with parents. Will these responses solve all classroom management problems? Obviously not, but they can help address many causes and situations that lead to student misbehavior.

The second part deals with issues related to challenging Jewish students in the classroom, age-appropriate methods of instruction, and difficult religious issues unique to the Jewish classroom. Jewish education is not a commodity to be acquired or parsed out in easily defined and understandable portions. Rather, it is an encounter with the Jewish tradition, which, if done properly, can and should leave both students and teachers challenged, shaken, and deeply introspective. A powerful, effective experience in Jewish education should cause students to question and, perhaps ultimately, reaffirm those beliefs and practices that define who they are as individuals, Jews, and human beings in an ongoing relationship with God. This part examines how Jewish educators can encourage and develop the natural inquisitiveness within all students; how to deal with questions that have no clear answers; how to treat issues of personal belief, morality, and critical studies. It also deals with the importance of incorporating prayer into all settings of Jewish education, how to go about establishing positive student-run prayer services, and, finally, the need for teachers to engage in a continuing process of personal Jewish growth and introspection.

The third part deals with the challenges of creating engaging and superior Jewish studies curricula and how best to implement them. Jewish Studies are far more than simply the aggregate of the study of Bible, Rabbinic literature, Jewish history, theology, and other topics. They transcend the content of their subjects and affect how students see themselves, as individuals and Jews. This part explores how to go about creating a superior Jewish Studies curriculum by analyzing the practice of tracking students with different skills and abilities into different classes, exploring whether Hebrew should be the language of instruction, whether it is more important to focus on text study skills or Jewish knowledge, or whether Jewish Studies courses should provide in-depth studies or topics or cover a greater breadth of materials. It also suggests ways to incorporate computer and internet technology into Jewish Studies classes, and finally compares and contrasts the various formats of Jewish education, ranging from full-day schools to supplementary programs.

Part One

JEWISH CLASSROOM MANAGEMENT

Sanctifying Jewish Studies

According to the Jewish tradition, the study of Torah and Rabbinic literature is a holy, divine activity. However, no thing or activity is intrinsically holy—it must be made holy. But how is something made holy? In Hebrew, the word for holy, *kadosh,* literally means, "separate." Therefore, things or activities that are holy are separate and must be separated from everyday, mundane, common objects or activities. So how can Jewish Studies be separated from other subjects? After all, if part of the goal of formal Jewish education is actually to integrate Jewish learning into other subjects so as to lead to the formation of a Jewish identity that is seamlessly integrated into the rest of student's life, how can Jewish Studies be separated out?

This same dilemma applies to the act of eating: it is one of the most natural, yet animal acts that connects us to every other creature on this planet. Yet, the Jewish tradition insists that eating be sanctified, made holy and separate, as benefiting human beings who are created in the image of God. So how can eating be made separate and holy? The Jewish tradition does so by insisting that Jews recite blessings before and after the act. Jews recite different, appropriate blessings before eating bread, wine, cakes, fruits, vegetables, and everything else that is edible. Once the meal is concluded, the "Grace after Meals" is recited to conclude the activity. Such blessings cause Jews to pause and take notice of the simple act they are engaging in and to thank God for the gift of life. Similarly, one way to sanctify the study of Torah, Rabbinic literature, Jewish theology and other Jewish subjects is to recite blessings before and after the act of studying.

Most traditional Jewish prayer books include a series of three blessings that were created by the Rabbis of the Talmud in order to sanctify the study of Torah. They usually appear in the preliminary blessings of weekday mornings. The text of these blessings is as follows:

Praised are you, Lord our God, ruler of the universe, who has sanctified us with His commandments and commanded us to study words of Torah.

May the words of Torah, Lord our God, be sweet in our mouths and in the mouths of all of Your people, so that we, our children, and all the children of the House of Israel may come to love You and to study Your Torah on its own merit. Praised are You, Lord, who teaches Torah to His people, Israel.

Praised are you, Lord our God, ruler of the universe, who has chosen us from among all peoples by giving us His Torah. Praised are You, Lord, who gives the Torah.

When I first began teaching Jewish Studies, I included the Hebrew text of these blessings in the student sourcebooks, which I had created, and instituted the daily recitation of these blessings before each Jewish Studies class that I taught. In addition, I included a closing meditation to conclude the class. While there are numerous texts that one can recite upon the conclusion of a unit of study, ranging from the Rabbinic Kaddish (also found in many traditional Jewish prayer books) to the various texts following the completion of studying an entire tractate of Talmud, I chose a Hebrew meditation found in *Siddur Sim Shalom,* the daily and Shabbat prayer book of the Conservative Movement, which is based on *Pirkei Avot* 1:12:

May it be Your will, Lord our God and God of our ancestors, to grant our portion in Your Torah. May we be disciples of Aaron the Kohen, loving peace and pursuing peace, loving our fellow creatures and drawing them near to the Torah.

I have made the recitation of these opening blessings and this closing meditation an institution in my classes. They create a formal beginning and conclusion to class. I have noticed many positive things that have resulted from these opening and closing blessings.

One of the practical beneficial consequences that has resulted from reciting these blessings is that it provides students with a few moments to get situated into class before beginning the lesson. Even before students say these opening blessings, students know they have the opportunity to take care of their own business. The pause that usually precedes the blessings often provides students with a few extra moments either immediately before or after the beginning bell rings in which to get to their seats, take out their note-books and pens, say hello to new faces in the class, and gen-erally settle down. Although it might take a few moments away from my class time, I have found that it is far better for the class as a whole to have this pause to make the transition from passing in the halls to learning in class.

Another beneficial consequence of beginning with the blessings is that I also don't have to try to get everyone's attention over a general hubbub of voices, chairs moving, and notebooks opening. I merely ask one of the closest stu-dents to lead the opening blessing, which everyone then joins in reciting in unison. This ritual serves as a natural juncture that differentiates between the time spent moving from class to class and the time devoted to Jewish Studies. The act of everyone joining voices together to recite a blessing creates a few moments of quiet focus for the entire class and aurally separates the noise of everyone settling into seats from the sound of beginning Torah studies. There is, indeed, some-thing sacred in the momentary hush that follows the conclu-sion of a group of people reciting a text together. What makes the moment even more special is that the students know they are reciting a blessing, a holy and sacred text that contains the Hebrew name of God. It imbues the classroom space with the sanctity of a synagogue in those moments, a spirit that one hopes will linger throughout the rest of the class period.

The closing meditation at the end of class also generates different positive effects. No matter when the closing bell rings to signal the end of the period, the students in my Jewish Studies classes know that class has not concluded until we all recite the closing meditation together. This is beneficial for two reasons. The first is that we are never interrupted by the bell in the middle of a conversation, question, answer, or comment. Whoever is speaking usually quickly concludes what he or she is saying, but the speaker is never interrupted by the ignominy of everyone immediately moving to pack up books and get to the next class. It is the group recitation of the closing meditation text that closes the class, not the bell.

Another beneficial result of concluding with a unison reading of the meditation is that it subtly communicates to the students that Jewish Studies—the study of sacred texts—is not to be interfered with by the outside secular world. The bell may ring indicating it is time to prepare for another class, but Jewish learning continues until we, as a class, conclude our business. Sacred space, once having been created and invoked with the opening blessing, cannot and should not easily be dissolved by outside forces. Only when we have concluded our business as a class engaged in sacred study and recite the closing meditation do students reenter the hectic normal routine of school between classes.

If Jewish Studies are to be taken seriously and made holy, if students are to understand that studying Bible, Rabbinics, or theology is special, then educators must take steps to insure that Jewish Studies are made separate and holy. I have found that the continued repetition of this blessing before class and the meditation afterward has helped to carve out sacred time and space for Jewish Studies classes, creating a sense of uniqueness and distinction that students should continue to associate with the study of Torah.

PRESENCE

I once observed a fellow teacher in her classroom lead a discussion from the front of the room. As the conversation progressed, the interest level of the students began to wane. However, as soon as she began to wander around the room continuing with her discussion, the attention of the students picked up. When she returned to the front of the classroom and stood still, the interest level immediately began to fall again. What was going on here? I believe that it was an unrehearsed demonstration of the power of presence.

What is presence? It is the ability of an educator to give 100 percent of his or her time, energy, and focus to students. Sounds exhausting? It is—but the rewards in terms of benefits to students overwhelmingly outweigh the expenditure of energy.

This teacher mentioned above unwittingly demonstrated how important it is that students feel that the teacher is "all there" and giving them her time and attention. When students sense that they are a passive "audience" they tune out. Who can blame them? It is natural for all of us to begin to tune out speakers, clergy, politicians, and teachers when we realize that we are being used as passive recipients of information.

Communication is a two-way street. Teachers cannot present themselves as the summit of all information from whom all communication flows downward and outward. They must also be recipients of information from the students in this communication process. Educators must be attentive to students' needs as learners. This doesn't necessarily mean that teachers have to turn every lecture class into a class discussion, although sometimes that can be helpful. It means that just because students might not be speaking up in class doesn't mean that they aren't communicating their needs to the teacher. The students in the classroom I visited broadcast their needs very clearly: they paid attention when they felt that their teacher was "all there"—in their presence and paying attention to them. But as soon as they felt that they were an anonymous horde, somehow distant, physically and emotionally out of reach from their teacher, they began mentally to "check-out."

Projecting presence is not a gift from God, although many of us who strive for this quality might sometimes feel that it is beyond our reach. Projecting presence is a learned behavior that can be developed by working on a repertoire of simple social and communication skills.

Physical Closeness

I feel uncomfortable when friends, and especially strangers, stand too close to me. As members of western society, we all have our own unique, individually defined although culturally influenced, feelings regarding how comfortable we are with the physical proximity of various people. However, this very discomfort attests to the power of physical proximity, and, like all forms of power, it can be used for negative, inappropriate or constructive, positive purposes.

When students get too close to each other or interfere in each other's affairs, they refer to this as "getting in someone's face." As teachers, our presence often extends far beyond that of students; therefore, we can often "get in the faces" of our students without intending to, even when our intention is benign or, in fact, positive. We literally need to give students "their space" to be themselves and project their own personalities.

On the other hand, the physical presence of a teacher can be a very constructive tool to indicate that he or she is paying attention to students. When the teacher I observed waded in among the rows of desks, her students felt her presence strongly. It communicated to them that she was "one of them," willing to participate in the discussion at the level of the students themselves. In addition, when a teacher wanders among her students, she reduces the ability of students to pass notes or go into the state of "eyes glazing over." The teacher can glance at notebooks to see if students are taking notes and determine the "doodle-level" in the margins of the note pages, which can indicate how attentive or bored students are feeling. Sometimes, simply being relatively close to a student can elicit a great deal of positive change in his or her behavior.

Eye Contact

Some teachers direct their lessons to the classroom walls or the blackboard in the front of the room, never making eye contact with the students they are teaching. In contrast, some teachers unintentionally maintain nearly continuous eye contact with only a handful of students, usually those who seem to be paying the most attention. Where a teacher looks can make an enormous difference is in the response of a class to a teacher. Making eye contact with a student sends a powerful message to a student. It literally says, "I see you and I am aware of you." Students usually react very positively to this kind of eye contact and will often return this attention by focusing on the class and the teacher.

Using First Names

I spend the first few days of every new school year expending enormous time and energy learning the names—especially the first names—of my students. I walk around the lunch room testing myself out loud, reciting each student's name. If I get stuck, I ask for hints, such as the first letter or the last letter of the name. I play name games in class, learning students' names in the order they are sitting and then asking them to switch places and have them test me on their names. It might seem a waste of valuable class time especially at the beginning of the year, but the pay-off in terms of the relationship that it allows me to create is well worth the time.

It means something to students that they are more than just anonymous faces in a classroom. The time that I spend learning their names and the effort I expend to use their first names whenever possible communicates to students that I want to know who they are and that I am interested in them as individuals. Most teachers end up learning the names of everyone in their classes by around the end of the first or second week of school. I try to attain that same familiarity by the second or third day of school because it is precisely these kinds of experiences that students remember in their first impressions of their teachers. It can sometimes make the crucial difference in students' academic performances and encourage them to succeed.

Praise

Do you try to "catch" your students being good or doing well? Do you thank your students for participating in class or volunteering their answers or opinions? Or do you take their involvement for granted. It might be a small gesture, but I have tried to train myself to thank every student who opens his or her mouth in class (for a positive purpose) immediately after the comment even if it is only a simple "thank you for your comment" or "good point." All students crave praise and positive reinforcement from their peers, parents, and especially their teachers. At a time when they are doubting their self-worth, even short, simple expressions of thanks can go a long way towards encouraging students to stay on task and focused in class. Even entire classes need to be praised. When returning tests or papers, I'll often comment, "On the whole, everyone did a good job with this assignment." Sometimes, I'll simply thank the class for a good class session and I'll specify why, such as, "We had a great, lively discussion today," or "Everyone came up with really interesting comments. Good job." Never underestimate the power of praise.

Smiling

I once met a rabbi who said that he occasionally practiced smiling in the mirror. He said that he wanted to make an effort to smile more throughout each day and he wanted to make sure that it didn't look forced or too much like a grimace. There are too many trite phrases that have been coined to emphasize the importance of smiling to add mine to the mix. Suffice it to say that teenagers, who are already over sensitized to issues of appearance, often attach great importance to the demeanor of their teachers. A stern or even indifferent facial expression can often inadvertently affect the moods of students or even entire classes. But, at times, a smile on the face of a teacher can lighten the mood of a student or a class.

Making Time for Students

When I am in conference with students, I don't permit other students to interrupt me. It is important for students to know that when they are with me, they are deserving of my undivided attention. When I am doing work at my desk, I try to drop everything else whenever a student wants to talk or requests extra help. The most effective way that we have to communicate the fact that our students are important to us is to demonstrate that we take their time seriously.

Students want their teachers' attention and in fact, they learn more effectively and behave better when teachers are able to demonstrate that they care by paying attention to them. A powerful way to do so is by developing and projecting presence in and outside of the classroom.

ATTUNEMENT

Do you know the name of the last movie your students saw? Have you ever asked to borrow the headphones of your students and listen to some of the music that they are listening to? Can you quote any of the more famous, popular punch lines of skits from "Saturday Night Live" or "Seinfeld" to the amusement of your class?

If you can't, this may indicate that you are not as "attuned" to your students as you could, or perhaps even should, be. Attunement is a term used in the world of psychology to describe the process by which mothers establish early, deep emotional ties with their infants. When a baby laughs, a mother may smile and laugh along with the child; when the baby cries or expresses frustration, the mother may make a sad face and lovingly echo the same sounds. Psychologists claim that, through such actions, babies learn that their mothers are cognizant of their inner emotional life and thus they learn to bond with their mothers and feel safe in the outside world. The ties that are established are deep and lifelong.

Teachers also must learn to attune themselves to their students in order to strengthen the learning environment in the classroom. Most students, especially teenagers, usually begin to let down some of their inner barriers only when they recognize that their teachers are aware of who they are as people and as individuals. Learning about common interests, likes and dislikes, and general background about people helps us to establish ties and build acquaintances and friendships. Teachers need to establish these ties with teenagers because teachers have the potential to affect the very way in which their students, especially teens, perceive the world. Just as a rope bridge is strengthened by increasing the number of connections between the two sides, the greater number of ties that we can create increases the amount and depth of mutual communication. Such connections establish the bridges between teachers and students that strengthen the bonds of communication and understanding.

Attunement doesn't have to consume an enormous amount of a teacher's time or energy. Simply by living in the same culture, teachers and students already share many ties. However, due to age differences, fashion changes, and fads, teachers should exert some effort towards getting to know their students; particularly in the following areas:

Music

What kind of music do your students listen to? Ask them. Borrow a student's tape or CD sometime and bring it home and listen to it while preparing dinner. Is the music upbeat and full of life? Or is it dark, foreboding, and melancholy? The kinds of music teenagers listen to often mirror the state of their inner, emotional lives. Can you understand the lyrics? Ask your students to explain the lyrics to you. What do they see in them? Do they like the words or the music better? You also might lend one of your favorite cassettes or CD's to your students so that they can listen to some of your music. Ask your students if, or how, they relate to their favorite music as Jews or from the perspective of the Jewish tradition. Do the lyrics or the ideas support or contradict Jewish values? Have your students help you to analyze the lyrics and values from a Jewish perspective.

Movies

What kinds of films do your students go to see in theaters? What do they rent to view at home? What are their tastes— drama, action, comedy, or sci-fi? Screen the movies yourself and ask your students what they liked or disliked about them. What are the values that your students are absorbing from these movies? Are they aware of them? Can they identify them? Do they really share these values, or are they foreign to them? Are these values Jewish values or do they actually conflict and contradict Jewish values? Ask for recommendations about what to see or rent and share some of your own choices. Learning to identify and appreciate the esthetic values of each other is a powerful way to create ties. Helping your students perceive and evaluate the moral messages of movies is also a great way to inject a Jewish perspective into your students' everyday lives.

Television

What shows do your students watch or record? Cop shows? Teen shows? Sit-coms? Soaps? Music videos? Talk shows? Late night TV? Watching TV shows is the best and quickest way to discover what the current fads and fashions are and to see what is considered hip. It allows you to participate in the jokes and sayings going around the student body. I once overhead some students relating what had happened in a sketch on "Saturday Night Live" and I chimed in with the punch line at the appropriate moment. The students were surprised and roared in appreciation of the humor and the delight of their teacher enjoying the same lowbrow comedy. Sometimes I ask my students about the Jewish content or values of TV shows. With Jews and Judaism becoming ever more conspicuous in the popular culture, more and more television shows deal with explicitly Jewish topics and characters. Help your students recognize these themes and to evaluate them.

Books

Do your students read books on their own outside of school assignments? What kinds of books do they read? Invest some time and read some of their favorite books. One student kept lending me her favorite books over a period of some months, which enabled us to have wonderfully deep and insightful conversations. Do you have any favorite Jewish books that you think your students might enjoy? If so, recommend them. There are many popular novels written for children and young adults that incorporate Jewish ideas or themes. Sometimes students develop a spark of interest in Jewish history or the Jewish religion based on their own personal reading. This is an approach well worth pursuing.

Magazines

What are the popular teen magazines that the girls read and pass around? What ads are they noticing or being affected by? What are the magazines or cartoons that the boys are reading and trading among themselves. Ask to borrow them and look through them. Ask your students to articulate the values that they understand the ads or articles to be communicating. Can they even articulate them? If so, do they agree with these values? Do they want to live their lives according to these values? If they can't identify the values, bring some of the articles and ads into the classroom and create a lesson that may help the students become aware of the media messages in their favorite magazines.

Web Sites

Are your students computer-savvy? Do they surf the World Wide Web? If so, what are their favorite sites? Where do they visit most often? What do they enjoy about visiting these sites? Visit these pages yourself and see what attracts them. Many of your students might even have their own home pages that you can visit. Send them some e-mail simply saying "hi." You might even consider creating your own web page for your students to visit. Cultivating an interest in the internet is a great way to connect with students who are growing up as much at home on-line as they are anywhere else. Share with your students some Jewish web sites or sites in or about Israel. As a sophisticated, technologically savvy country, Israel is a leader in the development of computer programs and internet technology. Maybe Jewish cyberspace will be the area that most attracts the interest of your students.

The ultimate goal of attunement is for students and teachers to see each other as real people with their own unique talents and interests. By investing some time in exploring the interests of their students, teachers can potentially create powerful new bonds of understanding and communication. Especially in a Jewish classroom, the more "real" teachers are to their students, the greater is the likelihood that the teachers will be able to teach more effectively in the classroom. And the more that teachers can become attuned to their students, the greater are the levels—and volume—of communication and learning.

Challenging Authority

"That is such b___ ___!" a student blurted out in the middle of my sentence, tears streaming down her face. The rest of the class, stunned, studiously avoided eye contact with one another and sat in an embarrassed, self-conscious silence.

"This really isn't the most appropriate place or time to discuss your paper," I replied to this student calmly. She shifted uncomfortably in her chair and cried out yet again, "The grade you gave me was so unfair!" She then proceeded to explain exactly why the grade that she had received was unfair. Although she continued to challenge the grade on her paper, she did so without resorting to curse words anymore.

When she had finished, I repeated myself that this was not the best time or place for this kind of discussion. I then calmly invited her to speak with me after class in the faculty room where we could better address the issues she was raising. Whether it was the fact that I issued her an invitation to talk about her complaints or the calm, unruffled tone I managed to convey, the student calmed down dramatically within a few moments. The tears dried up and the redness of her face subsided and returned to its normal coloring. I breathed an inward sigh of relief and picked up the group discussion where we had last left off. The other students seemed only too happy to resume our class conversation.

There are appropriate and inappropriate ways to challenge authority in an educational setting. This student was unhappy about her grade on a paper that had just been returned to her; however, she let her emotions overwhelm her better instincts. As the class discussion continued, the injustice that she felt bubbled up inside her until she could no longer stand it. Although the way she chose to express her complaint was inappropriate, it was typical of how many teenagers react when confronted with situations that they find intolerable.

Many of the discipline issues and management problems that teachers face in the classroom environment are typical age-appropriate behaviors. High school, or the early teen, years is the time when young people are beginning to explore who they are as individuals. As their bodies are changing and developing, outgrowing their clothes and self-images formed in their childhood, they are also struggling to adapt to a new social world with complex, perplexing, different expectations. They are still not sure of who they are or who they will be or even want to be. As they enter early adulthood, it is only natural that teenagers should be exploring to what extent they can act as adults. However, they often have no idea of how to act as adults. Being an adult, in the eyes of teenagers, can often mean being taken seriously and having an impact on their social environment. Therefore, they are exploring different ways to express themselves as "adults," which often means that they will come to challenge the authority of teachers and administrators. Although this may be an uncomfortable process for teachers (and parents!), it is a natural and inevitable development. It is also a development to be encouraged and welcomed within an appropriate framework.

Our popular culture also encourages acts of defiance and provocation. Television, movies, and, especially, popular music, convey the message that teenagers should be challenging authority figures in their lives. Song lyrics often idealize defiance, and *The Catcher in the Rye* is a popular book among teenagers not only because it is often assigned reading in English classes, but because it directly addresses issues of teen rebellion. Challenging authority is a natural part of teenage development, which is reinforced by popular media and the youth culture. Given this reality, educators must seize this as an opportunity to teach teenagers *how* to challenge authority figures in their lives in appropriate ways, through both direct instruction and modeling.

The most difficult defiant behaviors to deal with are also, unfortunately (or, perhaps, obviously), the most common ways in which teenagers challenge authority:

Public Outbursts

Teenagers usually have rich, private lives with much time spent in agonized introspection and critical self-assessment, which is why they need a greater sense of themselves in a public setting. As in the example above, this student was unable to stand the idea of living with her feelings of injustice being kept bottled up inside, not matter how temporary this may have been. She felt the need to express her outrage in public, before her peers and classmates. Had she dealt with her issues in a private forum, this would have deprived her of the opportunity to explore her public persona. Therefore, she needed to express herself in public.

Cursing

One of the most accessible and easily challenged boundaries is that of language. Children learn at an early age that, depending upon their vocabulary, they can influence the reactions of other people far beyond what they were capable of achieving previously. Using curse words is a simple means of challenging authority—in a sense, daring the teacher or administrator to take action. Curse words themselves seem to have a force beyond their mere meanings and assume the aura of verbal weapons.

Personal Invective Directed At the Teacher

Teenagers often have difficulty distinguishing between attacking ideas and attacking people. In their minds, to attack the person is to attack the idea he or she is espousing. Similarly, to attack the ideas that offend them, they feel they must attack the personality and character traits of the person expressing the offending ideas. Therefore, expressions of anger and frustration with policies or grades often come out as *ad hominum* criticisms of teachers and administrators. In addition, it is typical of young adults to personalize their animosity and focus it on the closest figure of authority whether or not this person was involved in the particular incident. In the military, injuring civilians is euphemistically referred to as "collateral damage," and in the world of teenage hostility, innocent bystanders and authority figures are often unintentionally affected by this "collateral damage" of teenage temper

While it is important to discourage these inappropriate displays of hostility and teach teenagers how to express their feelings of anger and outrage better and more effectively, it actually is important to encourage teenagers to continue to challenge what they perceive to be unjust in their lives. This encouragement is important because it can foster independence and assertiveness in teenagers. As young adults struggle against peer pressure and the desire to fit in with crowds by creating and expressing themselves as individuals, it is also important for young adults to develop a mature poise and the desire to stand up for what they believe to be right and moral. Encouraging the protestation of injustice is a crucial aspect of the Jewish tradition as well. Not only is the ability to protest injustice a foundation of democracy, it is vital for teenagers in order to mature into self-confident adults. The issue is how they choose to express themselves. In other words, what is the best and most effective way to express feelings of inequity.

The Jewish tradition provides much guidance in this area. The Torah states, "You shall not hate your kinsfolk in your heart. Reprove your kinsman but incur no guilt because of him. You shall not take vengeance or bear a grudge against your countrymen. Love your fellow as yourself: I am the Lord" (Leviticus 19:17–18). These verses, and even the clauses in these verses, are not placed in this sequence haphazardly. Rather, they can be understood to form a flowchart of behavior and consequences. Here is how these verses can be understood according to the Rabbinic tradition:

1. *"You shall not hate your kinsfolk in your heart"*—This means that should someone do something that angers us, the Torah tells us that we are not permitted simply to remain passive and hate this person quietly, privately, in the deepest recesses of our hearts. Instead, the next clause of this verse provides us with guidance as to how to deal with our pent up hostility.

2. *"Reprove your kinsman"*—We should try to rebuke this person who angered us; maybe what they said or did was a mistake, or perhaps they didn't intend it. The best possible result from this action is that this person will recognize the hurt he or she caused and will apologize.

3. *"But incur no guilt because of him"*—This is a difficult clause to interpret, but it can be understood to mean that we should not go overboard in our rebuke; otherwise, we may end up embarrassing the person we are rebuking and then be guilty of humiliating them. It can also mean that we have an obligation to point out

the errors in someone else's conduct and not simply ignore the transgressions we see.

4. *"You shall not take vengeance or bear a grudge against your countrymen"*—If we avoid rebuking our "fellow," our anger and hatred may build up to the point that we may try to take vengeance or a bear a grudge against him or her, which could lead to further anger and/or violence. This is why the Torah places this verse in this order. Seeking vengeance or bearing a grudge is a logical potential consequence of not rebuking someone.

5. *"Love your fellow as yourself: I am the Lord"*—The ultimate goal is not to hate whomever we are rebuking, but, rather, to come to love the person and, therefore, imitate God. This is the ideal outcome of this flowchart of actions and consequences. If we can successfully deal with our anger, we will avoid hatred by seeking a healthy confrontation with our fellow person. This, in turn, will enable us to restore harmony to our societal relationships, which is what the Torah seeks to create.

These lessons from the Torah provide a conceptual framework for dealing with issues that cause us anger or hatred. The question remains as to how best to implement such ideals in the real world. The following points, derived from Rabbinic sources, are lessons that educators can apply to students who need to learn how to challenge authority in an appropriate manner:

Challenge In Private

Oftentimes, making a public scene can prove more detrimental to a student's cause than were the challenge delivered in private. The student might become even more worked up by the public environment and amplify and expand the attack. Similarly, the teacher or administrator may lose a great deal of face and prove even more recalcitrant in addressing the concerns of the student. The most important part of learning how to challenge authority appropriately is learning how to be discrete.

Challenge Calmly

An excessively zealous challenge can undermine its very legitimacy and become the main issue itself. In other words, the way a challenge is expressed (its tone, volume, word choice) can become as much of an issue as the content of the challenge. Students must understand that, in these cases, the medium is the message. A calm and confident presentation can make a stronger case than one based on emotional bombast.

Challenge the Issue, Not the Person

Teenagers often are unable to separate an issue from the person who, in their eyes, represents the issue. Students must learn to recognize that often the very person whom they are most angry with, depending on how they present themselves, can turn out to be their most effective ally. The key is to develop better "people skills." Teenagers must be reminded to focus on what truly bothers them and not on the representative with whom they are talking. After all, every teacher and administrator should be seen as a potential ally in their cause.

Be Willing To Listen

In order to present a credible challenge, teenagers must be prepared to hear the other side of the story. They simply may not be aware of the motivations that have led to the situation they find unjust. Perhaps the low grade received was a mistake. Maybe some inadvertent action on the student's own part led to a poor grade. In other words, the situation might not be as one-sided as it is perceived. Students don't have to accept the reasoning or justification of the other side of the story, but they must be willing to listen to it respectfully.

Teenagers are not the only ones who must learn how to handle confrontations and challenges more effectively. Teachers and administrators also must be sensitive to their own reactions and behave in a way that will help foster these skills. The way adults react to teenage challenges to their authority can have a tremendous impact on how students will present their challenges the next time. The following are some suggestions for teachers and administrators to keep in mind when confronting student challenges:

Respond—Don't React

Reactions are the immediate, unthinking comments, expressions, and body language that we resort to when confronting challenges to our authority. The problem with such reactions are that they are unthinking, and their effects can be devastating to teenagers. Teachers may assume an inadvertent expression of impatience, fold their arms across their chests denoting defiance, or begin to attack the student before hearing him or her out fully. Such reactions are often visceral, emotional defense mechanisms. Instead of reacting, teachers must learn to hold themselves in check, pause in order to gauge their internal reactions, and then respond in appropriate ways to the substance of the issues being raised.

Remain Calm

In this case, the message really is the medium. Sometimes, the ability to remain composed and in control can have a calming effect on others. As human beings endowed with free will, we have the ability to decide when and over what we will become angry. Anger and defensiveness have their time and place, but when working with teenagers, it is usually best to remain calm and unruffled. Such reserve may soften and temper the delivery of the challenge.

Validate the Action, Not Necessarily the Substance of the Challenge

Teenagers often become passionate over seemingly irrelevant and absurd issues. Educators should take advantage of these situations to praise the students for raising a challenge, to admire the courage and the confidence of the students to express their feelings. The actual substance of the complaint or challenge may be groundless, but it is still important to encourage the desire and ability to stand up and challenge authority.

Be Willing to Continue the Discussion

Some teachers feel that the ability to quickly quash a challenge is the measure of their authority. However, just the opposite is true. The ability to nurture a challenge and find suitable, appropriate content within it is a skill that takes patience to develop. It also takes time. To develop mature and appropriate challenging skills and to be able to plumb the depths of any particular challenge take time. Continuing the discussion may take time, but it can yield many benefits.

Whether a teacher or administrator ultimately rejects student challenges, drops a policy or grade, or chooses to compromise, the end result may be irrelevant. When dealing with student-generated challenges, the process is more important than the issues. Such issues can be wonderfully instructive situations in which to teach a Jewish approach to learning how to challenge authority. They can also serve as a means for teaching and modeling appropriate behavior to improve the nature of civil discourse in our society.

DEREKH ERETZ

The idea that teachers are supposed to teach "character" sounds archaic; nonetheless it deserves consideration. Sometimes this is called teaching the "golden rule," but, in the world of Jewish education, the term that is often applied to the concept of appropriate conduct is *Derekh Eretz*. This literally means "the way of the land"; however, it is understood to refer to behaving in an appropriate, respectful, and caring way towards others.

Is it possible to teach *Derekh Eretz* in a classroom through formal instruction? Yes and no. It is possible to teach a variety of Biblical and Rabbinic texts that define appropriate behavior as well as provide examples. However, it is far more effective for students if they see living examples of *Derekh Eretz* in the person of their teachers. How can teachers behave in a way so as best to model *Derekh Eretz*? The following list is a selection of important behaviors that constitute *Derekh Eretz* specifically mentioned in Rabbinic texts:

- *Behaving in a courteous manner towards others.* Often, teachers are placed in positions of great stress. Striving to meet curricular goals, dealing with the myriad individual needs of many students, finding the time to prepare for classes as well as grade papers and tests would tax the endurance of anyone. However, if a teacher can make a point of trying always to behave in a courteous and respectful manner, this can go a long way toward impressing students with the importance of this kind of behavior.

- *Being careful and appropriate with one's language.* Why do people use inappropriate language? Stress and anger may provoke occasional cursing. Whether made directly or overheard, cursing can seriously undermine the moral authority of an educator. Therefore, teachers should strive to use only appropriate language in professional settings.

- *Putting the concerns of others before your own.* It is all too easy to become engrossed in one's own professional and personal responsibilities. Yet, one of these responsibilities for educators should be the putting aside of one's personal issues to help others with their problems. Making time to talk with students in times of trouble can have a significant and positive impact on students and demonstrate the importance of putting the concerns of others before one's own.

- *Showing respect towards others; specifically, teachers and students.* How can teachers show respect towards their students? By acknowledging their independence as individuals, respecting their choices, trying to accommodate the other demands on their time, and speaking with them in a respectful manner. Whatever a teacher might expect from his or her students should be reciprocated in kind.

- *Being humble and modest.* Egocentrism is an occupational hazard of education. When a teacher has a captive audience several times a day, it is hard to resist incorporating a sense of always being on stage into one's self-conception. That is why is it all the more important for teachers to have a realistic sense of proportion about who they are and what they do. Ironically, those teachers with the biggest egos seem to have the least impact on students, while the humble teachers are more influential precisely because of their modesty.

- *Not raising one's voice unnecessarily.* "Noise-inflation" is a reality of school life; the louder students become, the higher teachers tend to raise their own voices. Often times, however, using a quieter voice can be more effective and authoritative. The same is true when struggling to express one's feelings of anger without engendering anger among the listeners: a quiet voice is often sufficient.

- *Endeavoring to praise others whenever possible.* "Catch them being good" is a popular and appropriate piece of advice. A compliment from a teacher can transform a student's day and possibly even his or her entire approach to school life. We often only see the good in ourselves after others draw our attention to it.

- *Respecting the emotional state of others.* Some people want and need the company of others when they are upset or depressed, while others not only don't need such attention but flee from it. Because Jewish educators are in the business of influencing the religious growth of students, they need to be especially sensitive to the emotional state of their students. Teachers should get to know their students so as to gain a better sense of their emotional states and needs.

- *Being patient with others.* We all have our idiosyncrasies and personal habits that may annoy others around us. Depending on our mood from day to day, we may either overlook them or react unfavorably to the person because of such tendencies. Developing patience is a learned behavior, which educators should strive to develop. Just as compliments can inspire students, occasional, unintended expressions of impatience can harm the egos of young adults. Patience is not only a virtue, it is a *mitzvah* (commandment).

- *Being forgiving towards others.* Everyone makes mistakes. That is why it is crucial to learn how to forgive. The Jewish tradition asserts that refusing to forgive someone is considered cruel and unforgivable. The quality of mercy and compassion cannot be taught: it can only be modeled and emulated. Perhaps this characteristic of *Derekh Eretz* is the most important, because it is thought to be divine.

Derekh Eretz applies to a wide variety of behaviors that are considered "appropriate" in a social context. While adults and even children may have a sense of what is appropriate behavior in any given situation, it is important for educators to make a point of articulating what constitutes *Derekh Eretz* and model it as well.

"I'm Not Your Friend, I'm Your Teacher"

Too often teachers mistakenly believe that it is part of their job to befriend their students as opposed to trying to be their teacher. I have seen teachers request lunch room duty so that they could sit with the students and have lunch with them, or hang out in the halls and student lounge areas so that they could socialize with them. I have also seen teachers cancel tests and homework assignments or throw out grades in an effort to garner goodwill among their students. To be fair, teachers should be encouraged to have lunch with or hang out with their students and, perhaps, to drop a test or assignment; however, this should be done only on an occasional basis. Teachers should not encroach upon or in any way hinder the natural socializing of the students among themselves. It is also legitimate to be lenient academically when it is clear that students know the material—for instance, dropping a test or assignment as a reward for previous hard work. However, any attempt to indulge in these practices solely in an effort to become friends with students is not appropriate and will ultimately backfire.

Those teachers who actively try to become friends with their students end up neither being friends with nor effective teachers to their students. A fellow teacher once admitted to me that she hadn't given any homework assignments, quizzes, or tests in nearly two months because, as an insecure teacher, she was unconsciously trying to curry favor among her students. However, she came to speak to me about the fact that students were misbehaving in class and being rude and disrespectful to her. She was concerned that students were not mastering the material she was teaching; yet, she felt unable to test them for fear that this would jeopardize the relationship she was trying to build with her students. It was clear that this teacher's classroom management problems and the issue of lack of respect among the students were all related to her unwillingness to assert her authority as a teacher in her own classroom. Although this teacher seemed to think that she had befriended her students, the disrespect they showed towards her in class clearly belied this relationship. In addition, she had sacrificed her effectiveness as a teacher in her attempts to gain her students' friendship.

It is a teacher's job to be a teacher, not a friend. The advice I gave this teacher was that she should temporarily cease in her efforts to be a friend to her students and concentrate on being their teacher. As a result, she began to hand out written assignments and set dates for upcoming quizzes and tests and also instituted some consequences for misbehavior and rudeness in her classroom. The students expressed their dislike of this teacher to her face, complained about the new academic requirements, and tested her resolve at every opportunity. They understood what this teacher had been trying to do and cruelly manipulated the situation to try to punish her for ruining their "friendship." Of course, there had never been a friendship—the students had exploited this teacher's insecurity and played upon her fears when she began to alter her tactics.

Despite these acts of emotional sabotage and testing, this teacher held firm more or less. Students who ignored her assignments and tests began to receive poor and failing grades. Students who continued to act rebelliously in class or speak back to the teacher were sent to the principal and had their parents called. When the parents of these students learned of their children's poor academic performance and misbehavior, they began to exert positive pressure on their children to shape up. Even though this teacher was fighting an uphill battle, working to overcome months of ineffective teaching and classroom management, she slowly began to transform the environment in her classroom. Her students found they had no choice but to work to improve their academic performance, and the incidents of open rebellion declined as well. This teacher recognized that her overblown efforts at establishing friendship with her students had not only failed, but had cost her effectiveness and authority in the classroom. Instead, she began to recover lost ground and establish herself as a competent and self-confident teacher irrespective of her personal relationship with the students.

However, another teacher who sought my advice regarding a similar lack of student respect and misbehavior in her classroom proved unable to change her classroom environment. She believed that she had succeeded in befriending her students; however, her classes were little more than barely contained chaos. Despite our discussions, she was unable to recognize and accept that her own actions were the cause of the lack of classroom discipline. Indeed, her students did value their personal relationships with this teacher; however, they also felt uncomfortable with the situation. They were uneasy because they knew that they were taking advantage of an adult, their teacher, and were embarrassed that she was unable to control her own classroom. This discomfort also bred feelings of frustration and anger among the more serious students who were truly interested in learning in the classroom. However, they felt uncomfortable about asserting themselves by trying to encourage appropriate behavior among their peers. Instead, they felt they were being cheated by their teacher. While this teacher knew there were class management issues in her classroom, she was under the impression that everything was fine in terms of student rapport and that her relationship with her students compensated for the poor discipline in her classroom. Yet, it was this very situation that was eroding her relationship with her students.

One can be friendly, open, and compassionate as a teacher without trying to be the students' friend. In fact, it is more likely that an effective and authoritative teacher will gain the respect and possibly even the friendship of students. But this is more likely to come about as a result of instructional competence, not through the explicit pursuit of friendships with students. Once a teacher has established an atmosphere of mutual respect and a desire to act appropriately and has demonstrated an ability to teach, students will feel more comfortable with such a teacher, both in and outside of the classroom. Friendship can only develop in an environment of mutual respect; friendship cannot be purchased, at any price. If students consider their teachers their friends, that is great, but this should not be an explicit educational goal. The most effective way to become friends with students is to be the best teacher one can be.

THE MERITS OF *HAVRUTA* STUDY

Cooperative learning, or the ability of students to teach one another and learn together in a small group format, has been widely embraced in the world of pedagogy. This was long practiced in the world of Jewish education where it was called *havruta* study, or partner/small group study of traditional texts. In fact, *havruta* study has been a hallmark of Jewish learning for hundreds of years. While many Jewish educators are themselves products of this format of study, *havruta* study often seems best suited to adults or to particularly responsible and mature students because of the independent nature of the learning. However, when teachers instruct students in how to study in *havruta,* educators and students, too, can reap the merits of *havruta* study.

What exactly is *havruta* study? It occurs when partners or small groups of students read through, translate, and try to understand a text on their own. The purpose is to encourage students to pool their knowledge and build up each other's analytical skills. The best way to create *havruta* study skills is for a teacher to arrange the groups and give each member specific tasks. In that way, the entire group divides the labor of learning among themselves and learns to function as a team. In addition, when a teacher creates the *havruta* groups, this avoids the problems of some students choosing to work with only their friends and unpopular students or academically weak students being left to work with each other.

Among the tasks that the teacher should define and require from particular students are reading the Hebrew text out loud. Each member of the *havruta* should have the opportunity, and the responsibility, of reading the text aloud for the group. We all learn in different ways; therefore, it is important that students have the chance to read the text themselves and also to hear it being read aloud. Because Hebrew texts are often not punctuated, reading a text aloud can also help students develop a sense of the cadence and intonation of a text, which gives it meaning. This will help the students correct their own pronunciation as well as build up their aural comprehension of Hebrew.

Another important task is dictionary work—looking up the unfamiliar words so as to translate the text. While teachers will often create a customized vocabulary list with key or difficult words already translated, it is important that students of Jewish texts develop the skill and also the patience to look up words in dictionaries. This is not a simple task because it demands that students be able to identify the Hebrew roots of words, and have the diligence to search a dictionary entry until they find a meaning that makes the best sense in the context that it is being used. While using a dictionary certainly slows the pace of learning, it is an invaluable skill for foreign text study. *Havruta* study is one format that can help students develop these skills.

It is also important that students record the results of their *havruta* studies. Just because a text has been translated does not mean that the students will necessarily remember what a text meant. The ability to take notes while reading, listening, and talking is a crucial academic skill that all students must develop if they are to succeed in their studies. This skill is useful in other subjects as well. This is also a task that each member of a *havruta* should be required to fulfill. Writing is another form of imprinting information in our memories; therefore, students should not only take in data through their eyes and ears, but through their hands as well.

If students are able to master these skills within a *havruta* study context, then each member of the *havruta* should be able to produce his or her own translation of the text divided into a structural outline that includes any relevant explanatory notes. While this may sound simple enough, it is actually a complex product to create. The translation is perhaps the most fundamental and mechanical of the tasks that a *havruta* study group should be expected to create. However, once they have translated a text, the *havruta* members should then be held responsible for outlining the text—that is, writing the translation of the text in a form that reveals its logical structure. Rabbinic literature is often a complex mix of statements, objections, refutations, questions, and answers. Members of a *havruta* should try to analyze the text so as to understand and label each component of it.

In addition, they should try to explain the meaning of the text. Not all Jewish texts are self-explanatory, and the meanings of texts are open to multiple interpretations. The purpose of a *havruta* is to encourage students to develop their own interpretations of a text, share them with their study group, and even engage in intellectual debate to try to prove the validity and soundness of their particular understanding. This is the ultimate goal of *havruta* study—the development of higher order thinking skills and habits. Students in a *havruta* study setting must be encouraged and required to discuss the multiple meanings of texts, share their insights with one another for the mutual benefit of the group, and develop the ability and confidence to argue and persuade others to accept their interpretations.

There are many benefits to *havruta* study outside of Jewish Studies classes as well. *Havruta* study encourages cooperative learning, teamwork, and the ability to listen to one another. Because a *havruta* study format is largely independent of a teacher, students learn to develop greater self-reliance and trust in one another's abilities. Students can peer tutor one another and study at their own pace, which ensures fuller comprehension of texts and concepts. *Havruta* study also helps build patience and tolerance among students with different learning skills and paces. It promotes intellectual independence and requires that students develop their own text study and analysis skills. Students are often their own best teachers, and *havruta* study helps them develop those skills that are most needed for success in academic life.

The Need for Assessment in Jewish Studies

Some Jewish educators believe that students shouldn't be tested on Jewish Studies material because it will "turn them off" to Jewish learning. They believe that it is more important that the students "be exposed" to the material rather than to be held responsible for knowing it. Not only is this idea false, but it can be terribly detrimental to learning in a Jewish classroom and to Jewish Studies overall.

A fellow teacher once announced to his class that he did not "believe" in testing in Jewish Studies. His students were delighted with the announcement and acted predictably and appropriately: they did not take notes in class, rarely did homework assignments, did not study for tests, and generally began to lose interest and even express hostility toward the teacher. When this teacher came to me for advice, I promptly recommended that he begin giving tests. Although there was some resistance to this idea, both from the teacher and his students, once he actually began to test and quiz his students on the texts and information that they were expected to master, the learning environment improved. So did the attitudes and respect of his students. Although the details of the actual situation are far more complicated than this suggests, giving tests and quizzes played a significant role in turning the classroom environment around and making it far more positive and academically serious. Indeed, it has been my experience, as well as that of this teacher, that many students actually want to be held accountable for Jewish Studies.

Contrary to the belief that assessing students in Jewish Studies will discourage interest in Jewish learning, testing students in these subjects is an effective means to enable students to master material and actually motivates them to develop a greater sense of confidence and accomplishment regarding their Jewish identity. Why is this so? For one thing, testing students holds them responsible and accountable to learn the information under study. If there is no reason, or end-goal, for students to strive to learn the information, it is only natural that they will not do the work that a teacher is hoping they will do, nor will they learn the material. Schooling is a process whereby students are encouraged to transform extrinsic goals, such as working for grades, into intrinsic goals, such as learning for the sake and enjoyment of learning and self-improvement. Without testing or homework grades, it is unrealistic and contrary to teenage psychology to expect most students to be internally motivated to learn Jewish Studies. Giving grades, homework and testing, are means to help students internalize the love of learning.

Many educators who hold that students should not be tested or held accountable for the Jewish Studies information presented often attempt to encourage Jewish learning in the classroom by offering Jewish Studies "lite," that is, courses and subjects designed solely to be of topical interest to students. Some schools offer classes or electives in Jewish cooking, Jews in Hollywood, Jews in sports, a Jewish analysis of magazine ads, and other subjects designed to appeal to young Jews purely on the basis of their relevance or "cultural sex appeal." However, even if students are attracted to these classes, they learn the equivalent of Jewish junk food—they enjoy the experience and it fills them up but provides them with no information of substantial, real "nutritional" (read: educational) value.

One significant problem of Jewish education, either in Hebrew schools, day schools, or supplemental schools, is that Jewish Studies are not perceived by students as "real" school. Even in a day school context, depending upon the culture of the school, it is possible for students to develop the attitude that Jewish Studies aren't taken as seriously as general studies. The failure to hold students accountable for Jewish learning only reinforces the message that Jewish Studies are not "real" school and, therefore, are unworthy of attention and effort. With this attitude, Jewish Studies are not taken seriously. To counteract this effect, students must be held responsible for their Jewish learning in all formats of Jewish education. Testing and grades may not always be effective in nonday school settings, in which case educators must be creative in setting different standards of accountability. For example, students might have to earn the privilege of attending trips, participating in certain activities, or receiving public recognition based on their academic accomplishments or their enrollment in certain "core" courses on serious Jewish subjects.

A significant benefit of assessing students' academic performance in Jewish Studies is that both Jewish and general studies cannot be differentiated by students, and this conveys the message that both subject areas are meaningful and consequential. If learning in Jewish and general studies are treated equally, then students will devote similar time and energy to the mastering of each subject. If Jewish educators want their students to develop into knowledgeable Jews whose Jewish knowledge and identity is completely integrated into who they are as adults, then they must be prepared to hold students accountable and responsible for their Jewish learning. Only in this way will students get the message.

Finally, assigning homework, giving tests, and grading work are simple and effective means to assess students' knowledge and objectively document their progress. Testing and grading in the world of Jewish education can impart the same benefits to Jewish Studies as they do in general education. However, the purpose of assessment in Jewish education should not be to separate, label, and differentiate the "smart" from the "dumb" students. Rather, grades should be used to motivate students and impart the seriousness of their Jewish studies. Grading has an appropriate place in Jewish Studies; when it is discarded, the goals of Jewish education suffer.

Anything that is worth doing in life or learning and that gives us a rewarding experience takes effort, time, patience, continuity, and devotion. Learning Jewish knowledge, mastering Jewish texts, and training to live as a Jew are hard work. This is not always fun and games; it often requires concentration and exertion. But if we want Jewish students to take Jewish Studies seriously, then Jewish educators need to be serious about Jewish education.

CONSEQUENCES OF CONDUCT

Let's not fool ourselves: teachers can't force students to do anything that they don't want to do. In fact, to take this one step further, how students behave is not even the teacher's business—it is the student's business. The following is my official classroom behavior "mantra," which I often quote in class:

How you behave is your own business. You have free will. You can act however you want. But you must be prepared to live with the consequences of your behavior.

How students behave in class is their choice. They can choose to pay attention, take notes, and participate in class, or they can choose to ignore class proceedings, distract their fellow students, or disrupt the teacher. In either case, it is important for students to understand that this is *their* choice. No one forces students to misbehave or not pay attention in class. In addition, it is important for students to understand this is also their *choice*. The Jewish tradition informs us that all people have the capacity to choose how they are going to behave. We may think or feel whatever we may happen to think or feel, but how we decide to act on our thoughts and feelings is a conscious choice over which we can and should exercise control. Therefore, students are *responsible* for their own actions.

I formulated my classroom discipline mantra specifically to include a Jewish component that is rooted in the concept of free will and *Teshuvah* (repentance). Genesis 1:26 provides a philosophical basis of the concept of and practice of *Teshuvah*, stating, "And God said, 'Let us make man in our image, in our likeness, and they shall rule over the fish of the sea, the birds of the heavens and the beasts of the land and all that crawl upon the land.'" This particular verse doesn't seem to have any connection with the concept of *Teshuvah*; however, the Italian rabbi and Biblical commentator Ovadiah ben Ya'akov S'forno (d. 1550) comments on the significance and meaning of the term, "in our likeness."

S'forno notes that the word "in our likeness" can also be understood to mean that human beings were created so as to be *similar* to God, but were not created *exactly* in God's image. What is the significance of this minor grammatical point? S'forno claims that this term refers to the fact that human beings are similar to God in our ability to *act and function with free will.* However, our free will is vastly inferior to that of God's. For while God can choose to do either Good or Evil, God always chooses to do Good; whereas human beings frequently choose to do Evil as well as Good. Therefore, we are only *similar* to God in having the capacity to act with free will, but we are not *exactly* like God in our exercise of free will (S'forno on Genesis 1:26).

Teshuvah, or repentance, in the Jewish tradition is the act of turning *away* from self-destructive, inappropriate behavior, and *returning* back to the path of Godly actions. For *Teshuvah* to be possible, human beings must be endowed with free will. For free will enables us to choose between Good and Evil. Without free will, we would not be able to choose to do Good. Also, without free will, we would not be able to exercise personal choice and choose to do Evil. Yet, free will then makes it possible for us to disengage from doing Evil and return to doing Good. This is the function of free will as it relates to the concept of *Teshuvah.* Classroom discipline is directly related to these concepts of free will and *Teshuvah.*

Student misbehavior in the classroom is often motivated by a desire for attention—whether from the teacher or fellow students. Therefore, whenever a teacher stops his or her instruction in order to address student misbehavior, whether the teacher responds to the outbursts of a particular student or digresses from the topic to address the issue that the misbehaving student raised, then that student has succeeded in getting the desired attention. In other words, the student was *rewarded* for misbehavior.

Any time a student can successfully interrupt the process of teaching and learning in the classroom, that student is only further encouraged to continue with his or her inappropriate behavior. Therefore, the goal of the teacher should be to minimize the time and energy spent on any such confrontation. How long can or should a teacher spend dealing with any one particular disciplinary action? That is completely dependent upon the individual teacher. However, my rule of thumb is that if my attention and focus are diverted away from teaching in order to deal with a misbehaving student long enough so that I forget what my original train of thought was, I have wasted too much time attending to that matter.

One way that I have found to be successful in dramatically reducing the number and intensity of incidents of students calling out, distracting their neighbors, or others forms of misbehavior, is to alter the climate of the classroom so as to make the classroom environment much less hospitable to such misbehavior and encourage a greater sense of students' personal responsibility. I have done this in two ways.

The first has been to establish and publicize within my classroom an explicit set of behavioral expectations, a partial listing of positive reinforcements, and a clear and simple flowchart of negative consequences for inappropriate behavior, which I define in the section of behavioral expectations. While every teacher creates his or her own set of negative consequences for student misbehavior. Mine is as follows:

a. the first incident of student misbehavior results in that student receiving a warning in the form of a reminder to cease from that activity;

b. the second incident of student misbehavior by that same student in the same class period results in that student receiving a second warning and a short note being sent home to that student's parents describing the inappropriate behavior;

c. the third incident of student misbehavior by that same student in the same class period results in all of the consequences above, plus his or her immediate removal from the class.

I admit that my flowchart of negative consequences may appear to be abrupt and perhaps unforgiving. However, this flowchart works best for me, and I have found that I have rarely had to resort to all three steps, or even just the first two, more than several times a year. Usually the initial cautionary reminder is sufficient to introduce a new sense of sobriety into a student's classroom behavior. Thus, the publication of a short, but firm discipline policy helps to create a classroom environment that is less tolerant of student misbehavior from the outset.

The second way that I have sought to make my classroom less hospitable to student misbehavior is to deal with all such incidents of misbehavior in as dispassionate a manner as possible. One way to do so is to increase the sense of students' personal responsibility and accountability. Students frequently want to push the emotional buttons of teachers and watch them get angry or flustered. However, teachers have not been hired to put on a floor show for students. Whenever I have had to resort to my set of negative consequences, I have tried to do so as briefly as possible and in as an emotionally neutral tone as possible. And even when students are not misbehaving, I try to be as proactive as possible and repeat my disciplinary mantra whenever appropriate. In this way, I express my lack of interest in their misbehavior at the same time as I am acknowledging their ability to misbehave. I am not interested in polarizing the class between students and the teacher. I try to avoid creating a classroom where student misbehavior is seen as a provocation and challenge to authority. Instead, I want to isolate such behavior by creating an environment in which student misbehavior is instantly understood—especially by the rest of the students—as an individual's personal decision to choose to misbehave.

As contradictory as it may sound, I want to encourage students to understand that they can misbehave in class! I want them to know that they are capable of doing so and that I am not even interested in stopping them from misbehaving! In fact, I want to encourage a sense of personal responsibility in the classroom. I acknowledge the students' ability and indeed, God-given right to act as they see fit. However, I hope to create an environment such that they will see fit to act appropriately and live up to the expectations that I have enunciated in class. To doubt or to cast aspersions upon their ability to act in any way other than what is considered "appropriate" is merely to challenge and goad students into misbehavior and confrontations with authority.

It is the role of educators to validate students' right to choose how they want to act. We *want* them to act appropriately, but we cannot force them to do so or unfairly and inappropriately demand such behavior. Rather, we must encourage it and model it by acknowledging and emphasizing their ability to act as they choose. By emphasizing their ability to act with free will, we foster the formation of a sense of personal responsibility. And by reminding students of inevitable consequences, we serve to reinforce the seriousness of their personal decisions and we avoid the creation of a power struggle between students and teachers. We put the onus of responsibility back on the students, where it belongs, to challenge them to live up to higher expectations.

When students do choose to misbehave, then the concept of *Teshuvah* should be emphasized. By incorporating the idea of *Teshuvah* into my classroom behavior policy, I not only manage to inject an aspect of Jewish values into the seemingly unrelated area of classroom discipline, but also to encourage students to "return" to behaving in a more appropriate manner in the future. The importance of *Teshuvah* is that it provides a legitimate avenue of return for someone who has violated the code of appropriate conduct. Return is not only possible, it is the desirable outcome of a successful resolution of an incident of misbehavior. When students have been warned of their misbehavior or, indeed, have suffered the consequences of their actions, by teaching and practicing *Teshuvah* as a component of my classroom behavior policy, I hope to encourage them to make better use of their free will and "return" to acting appropriately again. Indeed, I bear such students no grudge, and I strive to positively reinforce their decision.

By my teaching and emphasizing the concept of free will, students are confronted with the internal challenge of having to decide for themselves that path of behavior they are going to follow. They may choose to behave appropriately in class, in which case it is vital to positively reinforce such behavior. On the other hand, some students will prove unable to restrain themselves and act inappropriately in class, in which case it is important that negative consequences be enacted immediately and dispassionately. Ironically, the expeditious and dispassionate dispensation of such negative consequences can potentially yield such positive results as avoiding personal power struggles and reinforcing a sense of personal responsibility. The act of returning, or *Teshuvah*, should be the ultimate goal of any discipline policy. Purely punitive measures only serve to reinforce that which is negative, unhealthy, and self-destructive in our souls; whereas emphasizing responsibility and inevitable consequences teaches the possibility and attainability of change and *Teshuvah*.

NOTES HOME

"If you do your work, then I'll do mine." I tell this to every class of students I teach in reference to writing positive notes home to their parents. Most often, parents usually hear from their children's teachers when they do poorly in school, misbehave, don't prepare homework assignments, or fail tests. Although students are often excited about good test scores, that is no guarantee that the students will remember or bother to tell their parents this good news. Therefore, I have made it a policy in my classes that for all students who do well in class or earn a certain grade (usually an A+), I will write a note home to their parents praising them. I usually write, "Congratulations, Johnny earned an A+ on his last test in Bible! Please be sure to let Johnny know how proud you are of his accomplishment!" This can be quite a chore at times when an entire class does exceptionally well on a test; however, I stick to my word—if the students did their work, then I'll do mine.

It is crucial for teachers to initiate contact with parents and stay in touch with them regularly throughout the academic year. As invisible partners in the educational process, parents must be kept in the information loop and be constantly informed about the progress, or lack thereof, of their children in school. There are many reasons why teachers should work to maintain positive lines of communication with parents. This starts the relationship between parents and teachers out on a positive note and establishes the trustworthiness and credibility of the teacher. Although it is not always possible to do this every year with every student, I have made an effort to send home one positive note about each student to his or her parents during the first two weeks of school simply to express my excitement and enthusiasm at having their child in my class. This can help incline parents favorably towards the teachers early on, before any less-than-positive notes must be sent home.

Beginning a positive relationship with parents early on in the academic year prepares the ground for potentially negative notes to be sent home. All too often, teachers don't bother to contact parents until something goes wrong, such as students failing tests or not turning in homework assignments. These are not the best occasions or situations for parents to have their first contact with teachers as it immediately establishes an unpleasant and tense working relationship. It is far better to have established a relationship with parents before anything goes wrong so that the subsequent contact will be all the more productive. In addition, by having created this relationship early on, it is more likely that parents will have heard about any potential academic or behavioral problems before they reach a critical point.

Establishing and maintaining a relationship with parents also helps to reduce the anxiety both parents and children may experience upon receiving communications from school and teachers. Few schools have succeeded in creating and maintaining a friendly, ongoing tradition of keeping parents informed about their children on a frequent basis. It is only natural that families fear receiving notes and calls from teachers because they so often prove to contain bad or unpleasant news. Therefore, the initial effort it takes to found such a relationship is well worthwhile in the long run simply because of the gratitude, help, and support such teachers are more likely to receive from the parents of their students.

Staying in touch with parents also helps create a positive feedback loop in that encouraging parents in their efforts to support their children often helps them, in turn to encourage their children academically. Possibly the greatest motivating factors of students to succeed in school are the attitude and encouragement of their parents. When parents are uninterested in schooling, their children are far more likely to mirror this attitude, neglect their studies, and thus do poorly. However, those students whose parents are genuinely interested in their school work and grades are also far more likely to invest the time and effort required to earn and keep getting good grades. Even the slightest, most offhand comments at home can yield long-lasting positive results in the classroom. Therefore, the more positive information teachers can supply to the parents, the better the chances that such encouragement will trickle down to the children. I have often had students come into class, beaming, and thank me for having sent a positive note home to their parents. It was obvious that the child basked in the approval of their parents and this attitude and sense of accomplishment was not soon dispelled. And the better the students do in school, the more opportunities there are for teachers to relay this positive information home. When a teacher, or a school, views the entire family as being involved in the educational process, the greater are the results and the more powerful are the chances of positively impacting the entire family.

Creating and maintaining good lines of communication with parents also establishes a paper trail that documents the progress of a student should further academic or behavioral issues turn up later. Teachers often notice and suffer through a wide range of poor academic performance issues and inappropriate behavior from students long before they bother informing fellow teachers, administrators, or parents. As a result, students may have established a history of failing to turn in homework, doing poorly on tests, talking back to teachers, or disrupting the class. By the time a teacher may seek outside help or wish to escalate the consequences of the behavior of such students by informing the principal or parents, the teacher may already be exasperated. The problem may have been long-standing, yet the teacher may have to convince the principal and parents that a problem even exists. If teachers have made a practice of staying in touch with parents about ongoing academic and behavioral trends, they will have already established a credible record of the student's previous performance and behavior. The faculty in my own school have frequently unearthed a variety of learning disabilities and behavioral disorders in students simply by documenting such behavior and staying in touch with parents. Many children have been diagnosed and helped with their learning challenges as a result of such documentation.

Teachers who do stay in touch with parents must be prepared to confront the fact that not all parents always want to know so much about how their children are doing in school. I once had a parent complain about the frequency and detail with which I was writing notes home, unfortunately because her child exhibited clear signs of a behavioral disorder. Despite the mother's reluctance to acknowledge the problem, the principal was able to use the notes with more success and eventually convinced the mother to have her child tested and eventually treated. His behavior improved dramatically as a result of the school's insistence and intervention despite the mother's unwillingness to deal with the problem.

Should teachers call parents or write notes home? I prefer to write notes home because they actually take less of my time and I can keep copies of what I have written for future use. To take the stigma out of writing and receiving such notes, I convinced my school to create a generic "progress report" form that could be used for both positive and negative notes home. The progress report form became exactly that—a *progress* report. Only in extreme cases will I resort to calling parents, because I have found after leaving numerous messages and counter messages that it often takes more time to get in touch by phone than resorting to the U.S. mail. In addition, phone tag often exacerbates parents' anxiety about the reason for the phone call, resulting in unpleasant, protracted calls that leave both parties emotionally drained. It is also difficult to verify the content of phone calls afterwards as there is no objective record of what each party said. Parents and teachers alike are able to interpret—or misinterpret—the conversation as they are inclined. This is why I prefer to send handwritten notes home as opposed to making phone calls.

While creating and maintaining such an intense relationship between teachers and parents can result in the creation of a mountain of paperwork, the potential benefits of such communication far outweigh the time and effort in both the short and the long run. All schools should work to facilitate this exchange of information by creating generic forms and establishing a clear-cut procedure for sending out large numbers of progress reports. Such an initial investment of time and energy is well worth the effort.

THE TRIANGLE

A fellow teacher once described a parent–teacher conference she had where the mother of one of her students was extremely upset with the grade her child was receiving. The teacher tried to explain that the student had failed to turn in a majority of homework assignments, rarely paid attention in class or took notes, and consequently did poorly on all tests and quizzes. For these reasons the student was receiving a "D." The mother, however, was close to tears because she felt that she was responsible for her child's academic success, but nothing seemed to be working. She was so upset that the teacher, in an effort to console the mother, said, "If it were up to me, I would give *you* an 'A,' but your child, unfortunately, has *earned* this 'D'!" Sometimes, despite even the best efforts, some parents find that their children are not responding as well as they could in an academic environment. When this happens, are such failings truly the student's responsibility? How can parents work to avoid such situations?

On another occasion, several fellow teachers identified one student who, despite doing well overall, probably could have benefited from a little more academic encouragement at home. In an effort to enlist the aid of the parents, it became clear that the parents were either ineffectual or even apathetic towards becoming more involved in their child's performance at school. The teachers' efforts to persuade the parents in this matter fell on deaf ears. They felt that it was the teacher's job to influence the academic life of their child, not theirs. It is not that they didn't care about their child, rather they simply did not think this was a legitimate area of their concern. And if it were, they simply were unable to see how they could help.

These two anecdotes reveal two very different sides of the same educational issue, namely, that the amount and kind of involvement parents devote to the academic life of their children has a major impact on their children's performance in school. Some parents are so overly involved in their children's education that they stay up late at night typing their children's homework assignments that are due the next day.

Other parents' involvement in their children's academic lives is so intrusive, tension-producing, and negative, that these parents actually contribute to their children's difficulties in school rather than alleviating them. In contrast, some parents are so uninterested in their children's education that not only do they rarely show up for scheduled parent–teacher conferences, it seems impossible to reach them by phone either—even in an age of cell phones, faxes, and pagers. They are "virtual" parents.

In nonday school settings, parents' involvement in their children's Jewish learning may be nonexistent or even hostile. Many parents who send their children to synagogue religious schools can't read Hebrew themselves and are perhaps struggling to overcome their own negative experiences in such settings. However, no matter what the setting, it is crucial that all parents who send their children to some form of Jewish educational school be involved in some way in their children's experiences.

What kind and how much parental involvement is appropriate in a student's life? Any advice is contingent upon the desires of the parents and the age of the children involved; however, despite these variables, it is possible to recommend to parents three general guidelines that may help them gauge how much and what kind of role they should play in order to help their children in school. The academic performance of high school students I teach is fraught with more than its normal share of age-appropriate, hormonally based dilemmas; it is also burdened with the intense pressures of getting into a good college whose reputation—and education—will play a crucial role in determining how economically successful they will be in life, at least so the students and their parents think. The following are some suggestions for parents to keep in mind when it comes to dealing with their children's academic lives.

Encouragement

It cannot be overemphasized how important it is that parents encourage their children in school by being supportive, but without overfunctioning for their children. In other words, parents should praise their children as often as possible and whenever possible for any school-related achievements, great or small. Such praise will send the clear message that the parents are aware of their children's behavior in school and that it is important to them. In addition, it is hoped that such encouragement will foster a positive attitude toward school activities and assignments.

Such praise need not be restricted purely to academic results. It is also possible for parents to be supportive simply by showing interest in their children's classes and school activities. For example, during parent–teacher conferences, a fellow teacher encourages the parents of his students to ask their children the following questions each day:

> "What did you learn in _____ class today?"
> "That sounds interesting! Can you tell me more about that?"

Such a dialogue not only expresses interest, but has the dual function of encouraging children to describe the material that they have learned in their own words, thus reinforcing the lessons and further clarifying and fortifying the information in their minds.

As in all things, it is also possible to go too far in encouragement. When parents continuously ask probing questions about the academic performance of their children and display too much interest in their grades, this can have the effect of overemphasizing the importance of grades. Just as in the anecdote above where the teacher half-jokingly offered the parents an "A," it was clear in that situation that the parents were inappropriately focusing on their children's academic performance, possibly to the detriment of their children's schoolwork. Over-encouragement can almost be as debilitating as encouraging too little in that both can negatively affect a student's academic behavior. Especially for teenagers, too many pointed inquiries about homework and class activities can be counterproductive and can produce a tense, rebellious attitude towards school work. Therefore, it is important for all parents to determine, through experience, what amount and kind of encouragement is appropriate for their children.

In addition, many parents, in an effort to coax their children into doing their assignments, often take the initiative away from their children by offering to help them in an assignment in some way. While it can be tremendously enticing to students for their parents to help them in completing school assignments, it is important to be very careful in offering such help. Parents can unintentionally overfunction for their children, performing tasks that may be easy for an adult but challenging for their children, and thereby counteract the positive pressure that school places on students to mature and grow. Some of the most important goals of education are to build self-esteem in students, encourage their self-confidence, foster a sense of responsibility, and teach them to make the best use of their time.

Offering to type a child's paper may significantly lessen the anxiety and pressure a child may feel about completing an assignment; but, at the same time, it will eliminate the very motivating factors that might lead to this child deciding to learn to type on his or her own. Although a parent's offer to help a child can encourage him or her in school, it can also have the negative effect of limiting the opportunities for the student to act responsibly and independently. While this may be difficult, it is vital that parents resist the impulse academically to "rescue" their children by doing some tasks for them and to allow their children occasionally to fail. An experience of failure may motivate them to devote more time and energy on assignments in the future. Therefore, parents should encourage their children in school by being supportive, but not overfunction for them.

Differentiation

It is important for parents to recognize that their children are not mere extensions of themselves. While children are naturally the focus of their parents hopes and dreams, it is unrealistic and unfair for parents to expect their children to perform or behave in school exactly as they did or to complete their own unfulfilled academic expectations.

Over the years, I have noticed a distinct inability of many parents to differentiate their own sense of themselves from that of their children. Such parents may react to information about their children's progress in school as if they themselves were the recipients of their children's grades, whether good or bad. It is natural for parents to be disappointed and feel let down should their children earn poor grades. On the other hand, many of my fellow teachers have been shocked and surprised at the anger and vehemence with which some parents have received such news. Rather than accept this with equanimity or with solicitations for advice and help, many parents inappropriately lash out at the teachers. What makes such reactions so potent and devastating for educators is that many of these parents are reacting with the emotional intensity of childhood wrongs coupled with an adult's capacity to inflict psychological harm.

As in the anecdote above, the parent's inability to accept the poor grade of the child was an indication of just such an inability to differentiate between himself or herself and the child. The teacher correctly perceived the situation and attempted to diffuse the emotional intensity of the moment by injecting a note of levity. Such inability to differentiate can often lead to the parents overfunctioning for their children, as was discussed previously, with the parents driven to perform important academic tasks for their child so that they will receive good grades. In this way, the parents may successfully avoid crippling blows to their egos in the future by ensuring that their children receive good grades. However, were such parents able to successfully distinguish between their own lives and achievements and those of their children, such difficulties could have been avoided in the first place.

Kahil Gibran, the poet and philosopher, wrote in *The Prophet* that parents are like "human bows," which shoot their children, like "living arrows," into the future. The bow and the arrow are separate components, but each requires the other to function at the crucial early point of the arrow's flight. The bow determines the trajectory and aim of the arrow, and if the arrow has been properly fashioned and the aim is true, it will strike its target. The metaphor is clear and obvious: parents' involvement in the education of their children is crucial to the children's growth and development. But it is important for parents to be able to differentiate their own egos from those of their children.

Model Appropriate Values

Just as it is important for parents to encourage their children in school and allow them to lead their own lives, it is likewise important for parents to model the kind of values that they want their children to live by. Clearly, one must practice what one preaches; however, because students frequently share so much of their lives with their teachers, many educators are frequently put in uncomfortably delicate positions where they can see all too clearly the divergence between what parents communicate to their children verbally and how they choose to live their own lives.

For example, as an educator in a religious day school, I found it very frustrating to teach about the sanctity of the Jewish holidays and the importance of living a traditional lifestyle and then to hear that a student spent Rosh HaShanah, one of the more significant Jewish holidays, in Disney World on a family vacation (a true story!). Clearly, the parents were interested in providing their child with a deep and thorough religious education; however, their timing and choice of family vacation undermined this very commitment. Similarly, while many parents may stress the importance of personal responsibility in their children and encourage them to make the best use of their study time, when parents choose to ignore the academic calendar and take their children out of school for two weeks just prior to exams, such actions also jeopardize the integrity of this message.

When parents try to impress upon their children that personal contentment and well-being are more important than economic success and then spend the majority of their waking hours doing business away from home during the week and weekends, what message are they really sending? When parents try to impress upon their children the value of hard work and satisfaction in a job well done and then ply their children with expensive toys, clothes, accessories, and cars, what message are they really sending? When parents send their children to religious schools and speak about the importance of maintaining their religious tradition but then live their lives in flagrant disregard of the precepts of their own religious tradition, what message are they really sending?

If parents truly want to instill such values as personal responsibility, appropriate time management, a commitment to justice, civil behavior, polite speech habits, a reverence for religion, and a respect for family and friends, then they must be willing to live their own lives according to these ideals. Parents must model appropriate values and behavior if their children are to get the message. Children are especially savvy about conflicting parental messages in today's world and teenagers are especially attuned to hypocrisy in the world of adults. Therefore, it is vital for parents to become aware of their own lifestyle and ideals and to try to ensure that they are living in a manner consistent with the values that they espouse to their children.

The education of children and young adults cannot succeed in an absence of parental involvement. However, the kind and level of this involvement can impact greatly upon the school life of students. How much and what kind of role parents should play must be determined by the age and maturity of the children. If parents can encourage their children by being supportive but without overfunctioning for them, if they can differentiate their own sense of self from that of their children and make the effort to model appropriate values for them, such students will be well equipped with the most important assets for success not only in school but in life.

THE PARADOX OF PERSONAL INVESTMENT

Virtually all Jewish educators are volunteers. No matter how much, or little, they are paid, the vast majority of the teachers I know in Jewish education are there because they want to be. They are idealistic, energetic, enthusiastic, and they believe that their individual efforts can make a difference in educating the Jewish people about the Jewish religion. The teachers that I work with put in countless extra hours after the school day ends, as well as time on the weekends and sometimes entire summers, improving their curricula, creating new lesson plans, inventing new games and activities, and improving themselves as teachers in general. To a great extent their jobs are an extension of their lives and their values as Jews and educators.

Such intensity and devotion yield enormous rewards in the classroom, in the school as a whole, and in the personal lives of these teachers. Their students respond positively to these efforts with interest and enthusiasm in their studies. Combined with the challenging nature of an ambitious Jewish Studies program, these dedicated teachers can help create a general atmosphere of serious learning and can bolster the entire educational enterprise. Many Jewish Studies teachers are excited to be professionally involved in Jewish education and to be living their lives in a way consistent with their highest ideals.

However, this very intensity and devotion is not without its risks. Just as the success of a single student can generate a "lift" and feeling of accomplishment that lingers for days and weeks, the failure or hostility of a single student can destroy a teacher's self-confidence, bring on a paroxysm of internal self-criticism, and undermine the very motivations that brought these teachers into the classroom in the first place. This is what I call the paradox of personal investment, and the following example provides an excellent illustration of a fellow teacher who experienced the full range of emotions involved in this paradox.

A colleague of mine spent many weeks and months developing a positive student–teacher relationship with one of his more recalcitrant students. This student seemed to hate the subject the teacher taught and behaved poorly and inappropriately in class. However, on rare occasions, this student would actually participate in class discussions and, at these times, her contributions were often insightful and would significantly improve the tone and sophistication of the conversation. My fellow teacher was determined to encourage this young woman, but first he had to break through her disdainful attitude and other psychological barriers that she had erected. This teacher therefore made great efforts to speak to her in the halls and in the lunchroom, and he made a conscious effort to be especially kind and friendly to her. He hoped that the creation of personal ties would help her overcome her negative attitude in class.

It didn't work at first. In the beginning, when she rebuffed his efforts, the teacher was despondent and often spoke of his disappointment and feelings of frustration about his efforts to connect with this one student. However, slowly, his efforts did begin to pay off. This student began to speak with the teacher more frequently, came to his office to discuss her assignments in his class as well as other classes, and even began to share parts of her personal life with him. She became more attentive in class, was more responsible with her assignments, and even began to improve her grades. My colleague was overjoyed. He spoke with enthusiasm about his success in reaching this young woman. He planned to devote this kind of attention to all of his more difficult students. He also seemed happier at work in general as a result of his success with this student.

But all of this changed when one day he gave a particularly challenging test in his class and this one young woman did not do as well as she had hoped. As some teenagers are accustomed to do, she blamed her teacher and took out her frustration on him by giving him the cold shoulder. She assumed an impassive expression and behaved distantly with the teacher. She stopped saying hello to him in the halls and stopped coming to talk to him in the faculty room. My colleague was devastated. He felt betrayed and personally injured and insulted by her behavior. He alternately blamed the student and blamed himself for this unpleasant turn of events. His hurt feelings strained his professional demeanor with this student and led him to question his commitment to Jewish education in general.

Was this teacher wrong to invest so much time, energy, and personal commitment to developing this relationship with this student? On the one hand, he succeeded in truly connecting with one of his students. He made a difference in her educational life and she responded positively to his efforts. She improved academically and her attitude changed for the better—at least temporarily. And these efforts also provided my colleague with extra motivation and imbued his teaching with renewed vigor. He clearly took his educational responsibilities beyond the merely professional to the personal. This kind of commitment is admirable and even worthy of emulation.

However, it clearly took a toll on my colleague when the relationship changed. He took the change personally, and it affected his private, emotional life as well as his professional motivation. He felt personally betrayed by this student and this disproportionately affected his work. It took a few months for him to adjust to the new situation and accept the limitations of his approach. The key is to find a balance between such intense investment and a more casual, relaxed approach.

So how can one strike a balance in this area? One must recognize and acknowledge the opportunities that teachers have to profoundly influence the lives of their students but also understand the limitations in bringing about consistent or permanent change and improvement. Teachers, especially Jewish educators, have the ability to dramatically influence their students, for after all, who can ever know the depth or breadth of change that even a single teacher can effect? On the other hand, such influence comes at the cost of tremendous personal involvement of educators. All those involved in Jewish education must decide for themselves at what point they separate the sense of themselves as individuals and their sense of themselves as educators. Teachers who fail to draw the line clearly or in a balanced way risk disturbing the emotional equilibrium of their lives. Yet, without some personal investment, the ability of a teacher to affect their students is necessarily limited. As people and as educators, we must all learn to strike an appropriate balance that works in our lives. The above example of my fellow teacher illustrates the dangers of upsetting this balance and not recognizing the limits that educators must define within and for themselves.

Therefore, educators must be aware of investing too much personal significance in their professional life. Yet, they must also beware of avoiding establishing personal connections with students. This is a difficult line to walk, yet it is a crucial challenge that educators must face if they are to be effective while maintaining a healthy balance between their personal and professional lives.

Part Two

JEWISH EDUCATORS

ENCOURAGING INQUISITIVENESS

I once taught a Bible class in which I tried to demonstrate the potential advantages of viewing the story of the Garden of Eden (Genesis chapter 3) as a "myth," that is, as a story that informs us about truths in our world, about humanity and God, but is not factually based. In other words, it might not be historical, but it still has much to teach us about who we are as human beings and Jews. I did not require my students to adopt or accept this point of view, but merely to make the attempt to understand how such a perspective can actually help us appreciate the story in a new light.

As anticipated, this idea generated a storm of questions, comments, and criticisms. And I loved every minute of it because it indicated that the students were not only taking my lesson seriously but were challenged to apply their own powers of critical thinking to this new information. It sparked their curiosity and aroused their inquisitiveness. I patiently answered their questions as best I could, but I already knew that I had completed a successful lesson. No matter how the conversation was to end, my students would probably continue to think about this lesson for the rest of the day, perhaps talk about it with their schoolmates outside of class, maybe even discuss it at home at the dinner table. And if I were really lucky, some concerned parents might even end up calling me or the principal to inquire as to what was being taught in my class!

When I describe this experience to fellow teachers, they often react with disbelief and outrage to *my* reaction! I have heard educators argue that by allowing such questioning and criticisms in my classroom I am eroding the respect that my students show towards me, that I am creating an atmosphere of disrespect for the Jewish tradition, that I am encouraging misbehavior in my classroom, or that I am contributing to the general rebelliousness of students towards Judaism. It is clear that most of my colleagues react *defensively* to this approach. And, in fact, when confronted with similar situations, I have seen fellow teachers act in an authoritarian manner and attempt to delegitimize such student questions or diffuse criticism by suppressing such comments or even simply changing the topic outright. Such reactions on the part of teachers are not only inappropriate and unprofessional, but they are stifling to the development of a key quality in successful students—inquisitiveness.

When students react explosively or in a seemingly hostile manner to new ideas, it is often because they are being challenged and threatened on some deep intellectual or emotional level. They feel embattled and besieged because their previous assumptions are being challenged. Students who criticize new and threatening ideas are attempting to defend their sense of themselves and their worldview and are seeking to assert themselves as emerging young adults. These age-appropriate reactions for teenagers are a natural and necessary part of their growth and development, intellectually and emotionally.

The worst thing that teachers can do when confronted with what they perceive to be direct challenges to their authority is to quash or delegitimize these student reactions. Not only will it not succeed, it will only further reinforce the typical teenager's paranoid interpretation that they live in an "us vs. them" world and create additional barriers to learning that must be overcome. It polarizes classroom situations and creates a combative, confrontational atmosphere that can poison the academic environment.

A fellow teacher once shared with me a disaster of a class in which, during the course of a discussion about a Biblical story, she casually proposed that the story could be better understood as an amalgam of different ancient narrative traditions that were combined in the text of the Torah. Her students exploded in howls of outrage as they had never been exposed to the Documentary Hypothesis of the textual origins and history of the Torah. Not content simply to attack the ideas she raised, her students turned on the teacher herself and questioned her competency as a teacher and a role model for Jewish students! Given the social and religious reality of these students, their reaction was not surprising and could (and should) have been anticipated.

The key to dealing with these kinds of situations is for teachers to understand that when students challenge or criticize what they are learning in the classroom, they are not attacking the teacher but the ideas—even if they happen to include the teacher in their attack as well. As difficult as it may be for educators to recognize, such behavior is rarely intended as a personal assault on the teacher. It is educational suicide for teachers to try to "bulldoze" students who seem to react in a hostile, aggressive way into accepting new and potentially threatening ideas and interpretations. Students will meet defensiveness and aggressiveness with the same. Teachers must train themselves to recognize that such behavior is benign and actually a sign of inquisitiveness. Students of all ages don't necessarily have the maturity to understand when they are feeling intellectually threatened and may truly want, and need, to learn more about an idea so as to help them better comprehend the material and therefore reduce their defensiveness and antipathy. Instead, they interpret the confusion of their emotions as being under attack and they react accordingly.

Not only is such behavior relatively benign, it should be encouraged and praised! As professionals in the world of education, teachers must remember that it is their job to stimulate the critical thinking skills of their students. Such displays of student intellectual defensiveness are actually signs of success. Therefore, teachers should try to greet reactions of student negativity with praise and encouragement. Not only will this potentially diffuse the emotionally charged nature of such classroom confrontations, it will send a powerful message to students that it is possible to challenge ideas from an intellectual standpoint without imbuing such questioning with an emotionally explosive subtext. Teachers must learn to ignore the defensive, provocative nature of many students' comments while helping them to identify and strengthen the critical reasoning skills behind such attacks.

Not only should such "attacks" be encouraged, they should be improved! Teachers should also help students to build up their critical reasoning skills by asking better, more pointed and poignant questions. Through Socratic dialogue, teachers can empower students to identify the underlying components of their thoughts and feelings and focus on the appropriate, inquisitive impulses that have led to their speaking up. Students should learn not only how to ask good questions, but how to continue to ask better, sharper, more pointed questions. For after all, the pursuit of knowledge through education is formulated through such questioning.

AMBIGUITY AND TENSION

A question that I am often asked is, "Who wrote the Torah?" In order to answer this question, I must first answer a number of questions in my own mind: Who is asking me this question? Is it a child, a teenager, or an adult? Is the person Jewish? What is the level of his or her previous Jewish education? Why is this person asking me this question? Is he or she looking to confirm his or her own suspicions or trying to "test" me in some way?

Depending on the answers to these first questions, I then have to think through another set of internal questions. What kind of answer should I give? Should I give a long and detailed answer or a short, specific answer? Should I give a survey of how the major American Jewish denominations answer this question? Should I give my own movement's response? Should I simply explain my own, personal view— and will this only confuse the person asking me? Do I want to involve myself in a protracted discussion of this topic, or do I want to give a short, but definitive answer that is sufficient by itself but serves as further food for thought for the questioner?

Actually, I would like to answer these kinds of questions by simply asking them in response, "How much tension and ambiguity can you tolerate?" Or to paraphrase the old joke, "Why do Jews always answer questions with more questions?" (Answer: "Why shouldn't we?") In other words, every good question deserves another question. Encouraging inquisitiveness in students means encouraging them to ask questions. However, not all questions can be answered with one sentence or in a format that will be immediately understood by the questioner. Much in Jewish life depends upon one's personal interpretation. Whether someone asks a question about the Bible, Rabbinic texts, Jewish history, prayer, philosophy, or theology, most educators run through the same litany of internal questions as I described above before answering difficult or complex questions. Yet, the underlying issue remains, how much tension and ambiguity can the questioner tolerate?

Just as there is age-appropriate behavior, there are also age-appropriate methods of study and inquiry. As children grow and mature, their natural modes of thinking, reasoning, and organizing information, grow increasingly sophisticated. Simple answers may suffice for young children. But as young children mature into teenagers and young adults, they should be exposed to increasingly complicated answers, or even to the fact that many questions have multiple answers or no answers at all.

To greatly reduce the possible answers to the question "who wrote the Torah?," one can answer: (a) God, (b) human beings, (c) who really knows?

Putting aside all issues of theology, answers "a" and "b" are really expressions of what people may think or believe. They cannot be demonstrated or proven by any scientific, verifiable means (despite the fact that many people try to prove these positions). In fact, to try to explain or argue the merits (or flaws) of each argument only places a high school teacher in a role of an advocate of a particular answer to the detriment of the students' right and ability to come to their own conclusions.

The most honest answer that an educator can provide is "c." Who really knows who wrote the Torah? No one alive today can answer that question or prove the answer to the satisfaction of even the most discriminating critic. When teachers answer, "I don't know, what do you think?" to a question, they are putting students in a position of power—the power to think and decide for themselves. These teachers are also acknowledging their own humility and their human limits of knowledge and comprehension. Educators don't know everything, and despite the profoundly central role they play in students' lives, it is important that teenagers as well as children see that teachers know the limits of their own roles.

When a teacher answers, "I don't know," he or she sets a powerful, but wonderful precedent for students to occasionally feel confused and indecisive. Ambiguity and intellectual tensions are realities of our lives as human beings, and when educators acknowledge experiencing them, they provide a healthy role model for teenagers to grow into adults for whom it will be acceptable not to know everything and not to know how they feel or think about everything all the time.

I once received a note from a student at the end of the year in which she told me how much she enjoyed my class. She also said that I was the first teacher who said "I don't know" as much as I had. She had even kept count in the margins of her note book and proudly informed me that I had answered "I don't know" a total of seventeen times that semester in response to student questions. She was amazed by my candor and acknowledged that she had especially enjoyed my class as a result of my admissions of ignorance. Sometimes not knowing the answer to a question can have more of an impact than knowing the right answer.

How students learn to live with such tension and ambiguity will significantly influence how they will live their lives. High school is the appropriate time developmentally and intellectually and it provides a safe, caring environment in which to expose young adults to the complexity and sophistication of life. But all children as well as young adults should know that it is all right to sometimes not know.

UNEXAMINED BELIEFS

"Do you believe in God?"

"Do Jews believe in angels?"

"What happens to us after we die?"

"Why are Jews opposed to intermarriage?"

"What is so important about the Jewish people that we have to survive?"

These are typical questions that I have heard students ask in all settings of Jewish education. Contemporary western society is characterized by freedom of belief, but many Jews, uneducated in matters of traditional Jewish doctrine, simply don't know what to believe.

We all have our own belief systems—children, adolescents, and adults alike—whether we are even aware of them or acknowledge them. Even in the absence of having learned a particular creed, we have all developed an amalgam of ideas, which we have read somewhere, heard on the radio, seen on TV or in a movie, or discussed or overheard in a conversation. The vast majority of Jewish adolescents already possess a vague but comprehensive shadowy theology regarding life, the universe—everything.

The problem that can arise as a result of this reality is that when Jewish students are exposed to Biblical or Rabbinic texts that deal with explicit matters of belief, students often have very mixed but volatile reactions. Some react to the study of such texts with hostility because they believe the Jewish text to represent an "official" belief of Judaism that may be in direct conflict with what they have come to believe. Other students may experience the same kind of inner conflict, but, rather than attacking the text or the belief, they fall silent as they wrestle with the issue internally. Still others may respond neutrally because the text is dealing with a topic they have never thought of before (although that is rare), and others, of course, may find that such texts confirm what they have always thought and may enter into arguments with those students who attack the text. What can often result is that the students are more confused and upset about issues of belief and theology than they were before they studied the text.

How can Jewish educators defuse such situations? By asking questions and teaching students to ask themselves questions. Issues of personal belief should not be avoided in the classroom; rather, they should be articulated and elucidated. Often, students don't even know they hold various beliefs or how strongly they may hold them. Teachers should seize upon such occasions of theological discord and even conflict as opportunities to help students articulate their beliefs. Sometimes, the mere act of enunciating and clarifying such beliefs can lower religious tensions in a classroom because many disagreements and conflicts are based on misunderstandings of the subject. The teacher can serve as a moderator of such discussions and model an appropriate, calm manner in which to examine matters of personal theology. Jewish educators should be like theological midwives in that they help coach their students in giving birth to their own articulated beliefs.

Of course, without guidance, adolescents may end up constructing bizarre, even potentially destructive and unhealthy theologies. This is where the study of Jewish theological texts fits in. When I taught a Talmud class, I assigned students to write a research paper on various topics of Jewish theology. They were also then required to give a presentation to their class on their chosen topic so that they had the opportunity to learn about one particular aspect of classical Rabbinic theology and share their knowledge with their classmates. The following is the list of topics I presented to the students, but they were by no means limited to these topics:

1. Jews as the "Chosen" People
2. Sin and Transgression in the Jewish Tradition
3. Free Will
4. The Soul According to the Rabbis
5. *Teshuvah* (Repentance)
6. *Tefillah* (Prayer)
7. *Tzedakah* (Charity)
8. The *Mashiach* (Messiah)

9. *Tehiyat HaMetim* (Resurrection of the Dead)
10. *Olam HaBah* (World to Come)
11. *Gehinom* (Purgatory)
12. The *Yetzer HaRah* and *Yetzer HaTov* (Good and Evil Inclinations)
13. *S'khar V'Onesh* (Reward and Punishment in This World and the Next)
14. *Malakhim* (Angels) According to the Rabbis
15. The Revelation of the Torah at Mt. Sinai
16. The Status of Women in the Talmud
17. Demons in the Talmud
18. The System of Courts in Rabbinic Times
19. Capitol Punishment According to the Rabbis
20. *Gan Eden* (Garden of Eden) According to the Rabbis
21. The "Evil Eye" in the Talmud
22. The Mythology of Shabbat in the Talmud
23. Marriage in the Talmud
24. Divorce in the Talmud
25. Animal Sacrifices According to the Rabbis
26. *Kashrut* (Jewish Dietary Laws) in the Talmud
27. Concept of Ritual Purity and Pollution in the Talmud
28. The *Mikveh* (Ritual Immersion) According to the Rabbis
29. Ethics in the Talmud
30. *Derekh Eretz* (Appropriate Behavior) According to the Rabbis

In this assignment, students had the opportunity to explore a wide variety of topics in speculative Rabbinic theology. The purpose of this assignment was to enable students to discover, through their own research, the spectrum of historically legitimate Jewish beliefs that have been espoused by Rabbis through the ages. This list of topics was carefully generated and purposely intended to focus students' energy into research in provocative topics. While the paper was a research project, students gave presentations of their findings that sparked lively debates and discussions about these issues. These were precisely the kinds of conversations that I had been hoping to achieve, as it led to a natural and healthy airing of students' personal opinions and ideas.

Students were able to compare, confirm, or simply become informed about their own beliefs in light of the actual Rabbinic sources dealing with these theological issues. Even if they didn't agree with the sources (or disagreed), the students gained more familiarity and expertise with a broad range and spectrum of Rabbinic beliefs.

Because Judaism is based on the observance of certain ritual practices more than on espousing specific religious tenets, there is no official credo of Jewish belief. Despite the fact that the great Rabbi Moses Maimonides did, in fact, try to codify a set of thirteen principles of Jewish faith (which became the basis for the liturgical song *Yigdal* found at the end of Friday night services in traditional prayer books), these beliefs are still not universally accepted by even the majority of Jews. Jewish students should be exposed to the vast spectrum of Rabbinic ideas so that they will have a frame of reference within which to develop their own personal theologies.

Students should not only be encouraged to discuss issues of personal beliefs in the classroom and write research papers about traditional topics in Jewish theology, they should also be encouraged (or even required) to write about their theologies. The very act of sitting down to write about God and the purpose of life can be extremely challenging and even frustrating to students. Writing requires a coherent and consistent approach to a topic of belief, but our beliefs are rarely coherent and consistent. While attempting to outline and explain deeply held, personal beliefs about justice in the world and existence of life after death can be a bewildering experience, it can also be profoundly rewarding. Not only can such endeavors potentially yield theological clarity, it can help sensitize students to spirituality in their own lives. The contemplation of the divine and things spiritual can also serve as a much needed antidote to the materialistic world of many teenagers.

Young Jews should be encouraged to explore all facets of Jewish theology in order to create their own personal construct of Jewish beliefs. However, it is important to remember that a crucial component in devising a personal theology is asking questions and thinking critically. Socrates is famous for having declared that "the unexamined life is not worth living." Jewish educators should apply this assessment to the world of Jewish theology and declare that unexamined and unchallenged beliefs are not worth holding. If the rarely pondered beliefs of young Jews cannot stand up to inquisitive, honest inquiry and questioning, then such beliefs are best discarded or modified. It is more important that students learn to ask thoughtful and insightful questions than it is to devise airtight, philosophically consistent and coherent answers. This is not because the answers are unimportant, but, rather, because the answers rarely stay the same.

Theological beliefs inevitably change as we mature. The ideas that motivate adolescents gradually and inevitably alter as they grow older. And the beliefs that sustain young adults often fall by the wayside because the spiritual needs of individuals change as they grow into full maturity. Therefore, students must be taught how to be lifelong questioners. To teach them to be satisfied with answers that they will inevitably outgrow is to condemn them to future spiritual dissatisfaction, frustration, and narrow-mindedness. Just as snakes molt their old skins every year because they no longer fit as they grow, so, too, do we grow and outgrow the beliefs and theologies of youth. This is why the answers are not as important as the questions and Jewish teenagers should be encouraged to explore their unexamined beliefs.

TEACHING BELIEF

A fellow Judaic Studies teacher once told me that she felt it was her mission to teach her students to believe in God and in the divinity of the Torah and that she felt responsible for instilling in her students a belief and reverence for God. While my goals may be similar, my approach is just the opposite. It is not the job of Jewish educators to teach students what to believe. Rather, their role is to present students with traditional Jewish sources and viewpoints and allow them to decide on their own what they are going to believe.

It is nearly impossible to teach any Judaic Studies subject, whether Bible, Rabbinics, life-cycle events, holidays, or even Hebrew language, without touching upon some topic of belief and faith. No subject is immune from such discussions. Even during classes on subjects not directly related to a theological issue, such as teaching Torah trope or how to wrap tefillin, questions dealing with personal belief in God, the divinity of the Torah, life after death, resurrection, the angels, the problem of Evil, and such inevitably and naturally arise. Such questions indicate that students are searching for some guidance in these complicated and subtle issues of belief.

Jewish educators should approach discussions about theology and belief with a great deal of care and caution. It is vitally important for teachers to be open and honest about their own beliefs and religious practices with their students. If students cannot trust or respect their teachers' honesty and integrity, then there is very little reason for them to accept other religious lessons from their teachers. Issues of personal theological belief must be approached carefully and perhaps even indirectly in the classroom for two reasons. The first reason is that when a teacher directly reveals his or her personal beliefs in a classroom, one possible outcome is that some students may either virulently agree or disagree with the teacher. Either reaction can seriously impede the teaching/ learning relationship.

My American History teacher in high school was a flag-waving, politically reactionary Republican. Certainly he had a right to his own political beliefs, and he certainly had an obligation to be honest with his students about his political opinions. However, the constant interjection of his political views into nearly all discussions, whether relevant or not, interfered with my learning American History. It wasn't that my history teacher was seeking to "convert" me to his party affiliation or political beliefs. Rather, he was teaching American History with a strong political "spin." Even when we weren't discussing overtly political topics, I felt the need to filter out the politics from the information that he was teaching. In other words, I felt that I could not trust my teacher to teach me American History.

Similarly, when a teacher in a Jewish classroom trumpets his or her own theological beliefs, that teacher creates a new impediment in teaching his or her students. Whether the students agree or disagree is irrelevant, but, henceforth, the students will unconsciously filter and critique all information learned in that class based on what they know about that teacher's personal theology and biases. At a time in Jewish education when it has become harder than ever to connect with students on a personal and spiritual level, the overt presentation of a teacher's personal theological positions can potentially create further obstacles in the fostering of the teaching and learning relationship between students and teachers in the Jewish classroom.

The second reason that Jewish educators should approach theological issues of personal belief cautiously is that many students are eager and thirsty for spiritual guidance. Therefore, they may be ready to adopt, uncritically and unthinkingly, any theological statements made by their teachers. I once taught about the Documentary Hypothesis to a class of ninth graders in an informative, tolerant, and intellectually open classroom environment. I tried not to color my lessons with my own beliefs; however, despite my efforts, I apparently was not as successful as I had hoped. After my presentation, when I asked my class if they felt that the theory that we had been learning had some merit, one student raised his hand and admitted that some of the information had convinced him that it was possible. When I asked him why, he stared at me dumbfounded for a moment and then meekly said, "Because you said so!" Even under the best of circumstances it is difficult to avoid influencing the personal, private beliefs of students. Indeed, it is precisely the goal of educators to influence the *thinking* of their students, but not necessarily their personal spiritual beliefs. Therefore, it is all the more important to encourage students to think independently and critically.

The irony is that, while it is vital for Jewish educators to be open and honest about their own beliefs and theology, the spiritual growth and development of students are impeded when educators are too overt or enthusiastic about detailing their own beliefs. Jewish educators' theologies have been formed and continue to evolve as a result of life experiences, education, and experimentation over a long period of time. Systems of adult beliefs evolve in response to learning and critical thinking. When educators prove too eager to share the results of our personal process of learning and critical thinking, they stifle such processes in their students.

It is a common experience for Jewish educators to be asked by their students, "Well, what do you believe?" It is important to refrain from sharing views too forcefully or directly. Teachers can direct students to other sources and invite them to return to discuss their own thoughts. They can issue open invitations to come and speak privately, one-on-one. Teachers can challenge students to reason Socratically through their beliefs to arrive at various conclusions. All educators must be extremely cautious about explicitly sharing their views with their students so as not to jeopardize the teacher–student relationship. By presenting their own personal views too forcefully, teachers may be depriving them of the experience of critical thinking and independent learning.

Many Jews have had the experience of being proselytized by evangelical Christians. Despite the outward respect and deference that such evangelicals profess to hold for Jews, they actually denigrate their intellectual capacities and ability to think independently. Indeed, it is the explicit mission of missionaries to influence and change the thinking and beliefs of their would-be converts. Whether the subject of the missionary's attention is a willing participant in this process or not is irrelevant, for it precludes the potential proselyte from having the opportunity to think for himself or herself. Similarly, whenever educators set out to "teach belief," they subtly denigrate the ability of students to think for themselves and deny them the opportunity to make their own intellectual decisions.

Jewish educators should not have "missions." Nor should it be an avowed goal to convince students to believe in God or the divinity of the Torah. Jewish educators should stress the healthy and legitimate role that personal theological beliefs may play in their and others' lives. The educator's role is to encourage students to wrestle with their beliefs and to help them to understand the implications of various options. Whenever students press to learn teachers' personal beliefs, teachers must insist that they share an equal responsibility to work out their own beliefs as well. And teachers must also emphasize the importance and legitimacy of being confused! Not all questions of personal belief can or should be answered quickly. Living with tension and ambiguity can help focus the questions for many students and enable them better to frame the parameters of the answers they may generate now and later in life.

Through the study of Jewish subjects and Biblical and Rabbinic texts, students will be exposed to a wide spectrum of historically traditional Jewish beliefs that, it is hoped, will powerfully influence the development of their personal beliefs. The study of such texts provides students with the opportunity to evaluate critically various theologies and encourages them to develop their own based on our tradition.

Jewish educators should be prepared to support students when they become theologically confused or spiritually despondent and legitimate their feelings of confusion and ambivalence. Many people are all-too-quick to think for us and dictate beliefs to us. Jewish educators must stand as a vanguard and encourage students to think for themselves. Teachers must respect their students' right to believe whatever they want to believe. And perhaps—because nothing is ever certain—if we have been effective in presenting the viewpoints and sources of our tradition, and we have been careful in respecting the intelligence and ability of our students to think for themselves, then just maybe we will succeed in creating a generation of intellectually open, religiously tolerant, knowledgeable, and committed Jews who will be able to share their tolerance and intellectual openness with their neighbors. And perhaps this will hasten the fulfillment of *Tikkun Olam,* the healing/perfecting of the world.

CRITICAL METHODOLOGY

The typical Jewish child's Jewish education ends with his or her Bar or Bat Mitzvah that, more than likely, focused on the acquisition of practical synagogue skills that the youngster may or may not continue to practice as he or she grows older. As these typical young Jews go off to college, they are likely to learn far more about Christianity, Islam, Buddhism, and other religious traditions than about Judaism in the course of their higher education. In addition, they are also more likely to experience powerful spiritual experiences in non-Jewish religious settings. Meanwhile, they may retain only a simplistic child's understanding of their own religious tradition and a child's lack of awareness of the spirituality inherent in Judaism. As a result, the vast majority of young Jews today possess only a superficial understanding of Judaism that cannot possibly compete for their spiritual loyalty or serve as a focus for future study.

To offset this widespread phenomenon, Jewish educators who have the opportunity to teach young Jews in their teenage years should seize this opportunity to present the Jewish tradition in the most vital, compelling, and challenging manner possible. Namely, Jewish educators teaching Jewish teenagers should concentrate exclusively on presenting the Jewish tradition from a reverential, but critical perspective.

Specifically, Jewish educators should not shy away from teaching about the Documentary Thesis regarding the historical composite development of the Biblical books. Nor should they ignore external sources historically concurrent with Biblical narratives, such as Mesopotamian mythology, Hittite legal traditions, royal Egyptian annals, and ancient ostrakon (writing on clay fragments). Hanukkah should not be taught as a mere morality play between religious persecution of the Jews by the Seleucid Hellenists versus the efforts of the Maccabees to ensure religious liberty. Rather, young Jewish adults should be presented with the historical difficulties involved in the fact that Antiochus Epiphanies IV, an enlightened, tolerant Hellenistic despot, acted totally contrary to Hellenistic culture and long-standing tradition in pursuing hostilities with the Jewish culture and religion. The literary sources of the Oral Torah (that is, the *Mishnah, Gemara,* and Midrashic works) should be introduced to students in all of their complication, sophistication, and obscurity. Rather than simplify these sources and teach them only for content, students should learn about all of these sources and topics utilizing critical methodology.

What does it mean to teach the Bible or selections of Rabbinic literature from a critical perspective or using critical methodology? Quite simply, it means studying these texts from more than one perspective. The most common approach to teaching Bible is to focus on the narratives of the patriarchs, matriarchs, judges, prophets, and kings or the laws of the Torah. The most common approach to teaching selections of the *Mishnah* and *Gemara* is to focus on those legal portions that help shed light on current Jewish customs and religious practices, and the teaching of Midrashic texts is usually supplemental to the study of Biblical stories to help fill in the gaps. In and of themselves, these approaches are appropriate and legitimate ways of teaching Biblical and Rabbinic texts. But by themselves alone, such simplistic, content-based approaches are woefully inadequate to excite the interest of Jewish teenagers or challenge their emerging intellectual, critical reasoning skills.

Teaching the Bible and selections of Rabbinic literature from a critical perspective means that teaching these texts for their mere content is insufficient. Teaching these texts using critical methodology demands that Jewish educators, after presenting the content, then subject these same texts to literary analysis, historical analysis, and theological analysis. A literary analysis of some Biblical narratives could possibly lead to the emphasis of certain points that were far from obvious in the content-based reading. For instance, when seen in their context, the actions of many of the Biblical patriarchs are far from exemplary. Rather than shying away from these problems, teachers should acknowledge and deal with such difficulties in the classroom. In addition, the historical analysis of some *Mishnayot,* or selections of the *Gemara* or Midrashic works, may reveal far different conclusions than a simple Halakhic (legal) reading. For example, when contrasted with one another, the relevant Rabbinic sources dealing with the origins of Hanukkah are far from clear or simple. And, finally, a theological analysis of either Biblical or Rabbinic texts may spark far-ranging discussions about God and morality than could possibly be achieved through a straight, frontal approach of such subjects. In short, it is quite possible that each separate form of analysis may yield different, even contradictory results. And this is the purpose of using critical methodology!

Teaching Jewish subjects and Jewish texts using critical methodology doesn't mean attacking the Jewish tradition or threatening the beliefs of young Jews. Instead, it mean broadening the intellectual and spiritual horizon of Jewish students, encouraging them to think through their own interpretations and beliefs openly and honestly. Conflicts and contradictions may arise, but that is only natural. Learning to accept and trying to resolve such conflicts should be an important and vital component not only to Jewish education, but to general education as well. The use of critical methodology means encouraging Jewish teenagers to realize that there is no single "right" or "wrong" theological beliefs; rather, there is a spectrum of historically acknowledged Jewish interpretations of Jewish texts. Studying Judaism using critical methodology leads directly and inevitably to the deepening of one's perception and understanding of the depth and profundity of Jewish tradition.

In other words, Jewish Studies classes should engage students at the point where they are developmentally in their intellectual maturation and should challenge them. There should be more to Jewish Studies classes than simply learning content; classes on Bible, Rabbinic literature, and Philosophy should challenge students with the best that the Jewish tradition has to offer. Judaism is a complex, demanding, sophisticated tradition with vast, challenging, resources that can and should be presented to Jewish students in all educational formats. Young Jews should graduate from any and all Jewish educational settings overwhelmed by the sophistication and wealth of the Jewish tradition.

The high school years are the time when young adults are learning more sophisticated ways of perceiving and understanding the world around them. Their powers of reasoning are greatly expanding. Unless sufficiently challenged, these new, incipient critical reasoning skills will go undeveloped or underdeveloped. Or perhaps what is worse—and is already largely the case—young Jewish adults will acquire and refine these intellectual skills but in other, general subjects, such as English, Math, Science, and History, while Jewish texts and Jewish subjects are perforce relegated to a less-challenging realm of intellectual activity. And worse yet, once acquired in general subjects, young Jews may apply such critical methods to their simplistic memories of Judaism with spiritually destructive results.

Adolescence is the time when students tend to fall in love with academic subjects for the first time. Such intellectual love affairs can determine the career or field of work these students will choose to devote the rest of their lives. As Jewish teenagers are going to be developing these critical skills anyway in their high school years, it is only appropriate that they should be introduced to critical thinking skills in Jewish subjects and using Jewish texts to stimulate their interest and capture their attention. Not everyone will fall in love with Jewish subjects or texts, but that really isn't the goal of applying critical methodology to Jewish topics. Rather, the goal is to create lifelong committed, intellectually engaged Jews, who, once challenged by Judaism, will forever be drawn to it.

Teaching Morality

"Abraham was a slimeball."

There was an audible gasp in the classroom when I said that. Perhaps the students couldn't believe that their teacher, a rabbi no less, had made such an audacious, irreverent statement. However, it ignited a debate about the section of the Torah that we were studying and led to a lively debate about the moral character of the Biblical patriarch.

We had been studying Genesis, chapter 12, in which Abraham moves to Egypt to escape a famine in the land of Israel. Fearing for his life, Abraham instructs his wife, Sarah, to tell the Egyptians that he is her brother in order to safeguard his own life. Our discussion was growing a bit stale as my students began recounting the familiar historical claim of many Jewish historians, cultural anthropologists, and Biblical apologists that in the ancient Near East, wives were often called "sisters" by their husbands (as actually attested to in ancient Near Eastern documents). Rather than enter into a debate based on mutual ignorance of this abstruse detail of ancient legal systems, I decided to explore the moral implications of Abraham's actions in the context of just the narrative alone. Maybe Abraham told his wife to lie about their relationship so that he might be able to profit from the relationship! After all, as the Genesis series broadcast by PBS a few years ago made clear, the Biblical patriarchs were not always paragons of virtue. The plain truth of the matter is that Sarah was taken by Pharaoh into his palace and Abraham received many camels and donkeys and slaves as a result of this relationship. I merely wanted to point out this disturbing fact to my students so that they might consider all of the moral dimensions involved in this situation.

The classroom discussion that followed was enlightening for a number of reasons. The first was that it allowed the students to talk about the Torah and Biblical characters from a completely new perspective in their experience. Second, the discussion demanded that the students consider the potential for moral ambiguity in the Torah; and, finally, the students had to identify and analyze their own moral reactions to the text. What began as a somewhat academic discussion about a distant religious text and event was transformed into a passionate, contemporary moral debate. The goal was not to arrive at an answer, but to encourage the students to evaluate the Torah as a source of values.

Jewish education should not be a process of "garbage in, garbage out," in which students are asked to master vast amounts of historical, legal, and literary details about the Jewish traditions so that others will consider them Jewishly educated. Instead, it should provide an opportunity to challenge and build up the very moral fiber of the students. Such discussions about morality should not be confined to an examination of the past, in which historical and literary situations and events are rehashed from a moral perspective A typical example of this anemic approach to injecting Jewish education with a moral message is the utterly irrelevant question, "Was it more moral for Jews to flee Spain in 1492 or remain and become 'conversos'"? While it is possible for students to engage in a lively debate about this issue, the context is far removed from American Jewish students' lives today. Therefore students should be encouraged to consider the moral implications of the text and historical reality and, obviously, the Jewish moral implications of all aspects of their lives today.

A significant example of how and where moral analysis can and should be brought to bear is in the area of environmental education in a Jewish context. Why environment studies? Because the science of ecology teaches us one central truth: all life—including human life—depends on all other life, and its continued existence relies on the health of the world's ecosystems. The Jewish tradition teaches us another central truth: all life is holy and humans have a unique responsibility to preserve God's creations. However, many ecological systems that help to maintain human existence are on the brink of collapse. Only an educated and committed population can build on the successes of the past in diverting ecological disasters and ensuring a sustainable future. However, environmental education by itself is not enough. While familiarity with such topics as wildlife ecology, the carbon cycle, acid rain, and soil depletion that students may learn in their general studies courses and secular schools are important, this knowledge in and of itself does not guarantee or inspire a commitment to ecological improvement. The introduction of religious, moral studies is a vital component of this education. However, a class that presents these religious texts alone in dealing with these issues is insufficient.

Humanity has arrived at a point in the development of our society where young Jews who are expected to grow into responsible leaders must be schooled in religious ethics, environmental science, and moral philosophy in order to deal with the current and growing ecological crises that they will confront in their lifetimes. This is simply one compelling reason why students in Jewish educational formats should learn about Jewish subjects, as well as others such as ecology, from a moral perspective. One such course that I have helped to create with a fellow science teacher, entitled "Living on God's Earth," is a model for integrating the scientific background of environmental science and ecological writers and Jewish sources and morality. Whereas public schools are forbidden from injecting religious values into their curricula, Jewish educators have a mandate to teach a values-laden curriculum of environmentalism and instill the ethics of the Jewish tradition in all the material that is taught. The objectives of our course are as follows:

To convey a sense of the wonder of nature. All subsequent learning will be in vain unless it is predicated on an appreciation of nature: "How great are Your works, O God, how very subtle Your designs" (Psalms 92:6). We try to convey a sense of the wonder of nature through creative writing assignments that require spending time outdoors; studying the complexity of food webs and the cycles of carbon, nitrogen, oxygen, and other elements; reading appropriate selections from writers such as Emerson, Thoreau, Rachel Carson, and Aldo Leopold, that deal with the splendor of the outdoors as well as the numerous relevant Biblical and Rabbinic texts that extol the beauty and complexity of God's creation. We try to teach all of our material in such a way as to reawaken a childlike sense of wonder of the world.

To inform about ecological perils. One point of fierce contention in the world of environmental education today is whether we are inappropriately scaring our children by teaching them about environmental disasters, past, present, and future. Our intention is not to scare our students but, rather, to inform them about the potentially deleterious consequences of human impact on the natural cycles, ecosystems, and wildlife habitats. These objectives build upon one another: for without a sense of wonder and appreciation of nature, there is no basis for being alarmed by ecological crises; and without a sense of the history of ecological disturbances and their causes, there is no urgency to the study of the environment.

To explore the wisdom of the Jewish tradition and our responsibility as Jews. Jewish texts contain an archive of values that are relevant to the study of environmental science. Numerous Jewish texts command protection of the environment and also acclaim the value of biodiversity, dealing with such topics ranging from the preservation of all species to the prevention of cruelty to animals. While an appreciation of the aesthetic value of nature and its despoliation can arouse outrage, the exploration of relevant Biblical and Rabbinic texts can provide a more grounded moral perspective on these issues. For example, there are many texts that seem to imply that humans should be stewards and caretakers of creation, whereas others seem to value the world only in its usefulness to humanity. Young Jews, as well as adults, must become more familiar with the wide range of Jewish responses and attitudes inherent in the Jewish tradition.

To work towards the political and social integration of this knowledge. If we have been effective, our students will emerge changed from their encounter with the material in this course. Thus, it is unfair, even irresponsible, to educate students about environmentalism from a scientific and Jewish moral perspective and then leave them to reconstruct their sense of selves without guidance and support. Students are required to write frequent journal entries in which they are encouraged to express their personal reactions to and reflections on the information they have been learning. Group discussions enable students to wrestle with related issues and concerns. Assignments include political and moral explorations of their emerging sense of themselves through interviews with family members and friends. One of the purposes of this course is to invite students to ask themselves who they are and who they will be. In other words, will they conduct their lives any differently now or in the future? How will they integrate this knowledge into their lives? The study of the environment converges with the Jewish tradition in that an encounter with both of them demands *heshbon nefesh,* or introspection.

The study of the environment is becoming a standard subject in our educational institutions, beginning in elementary school or even earlier. In addition, the popularization and awareness of Jewish texts that are relevant to the study of ecology is also growing in the world of Jewish education. This is important because it has been one area of study that is actually historically unique and distinct in that it has never been considered or even identified as worthy of separate attention.

What makes "Living on God's Earth" unique is that it is an in-depth course in Rabbinic literature. Students study the Hebrew (and Aramaic) Biblical, Talmudic, and Midrashic texts and the Medieval Halakhic codes that deal with such topics as early environmental zoning laws, property rights that conflict with the use of land for the common good, the limits of the commandment to "be fruitful and multiply," legal liability for causing ecological damage, and a panoply of other, related topics.

There are actually a number of very good books available that offer a selection of these subjects. However, these books are limited by the fact that they provide only English translations of Biblical and Rabbinic texts. While these authors and editors are obviously catering to a non-Hebrew literate audience, the depth of analysis of these texts is limited by this linguistic barrier. Similarly, while one may read an English translation of the Talmud, one cannot appreciate or fully enter into the transgenerational dialogue of the Sages without immersing oneself in the language of discourse. As a result, these English Judaica books on the environment are confined to providing a superficial presentation of the sources. While such sourcebooks may assuage many people or be able to provide a well-chosen quote to drop in a conversation on the environment to "prove" that Judaism has "something to say" about it, they are inadequate for providing a basis for serious moral analysis, discussion, and critique of conflicting Jewish values regarding the environment. The study of Rabbinic sources provides an opportunity to explore the spectrum of values that the Jewish tradition assigns to nature, wildlife, and human exploitation of these resources. It also enables students to identify their own conscious and subconscious attitudes towards nature and humanity.

The course, "Living on God's Earth," encourages students to construct their own environmental theologies free from coercion and political propaganda. When we first proposed this course to the administration in our school, there was some concern that this class might become a forum in which we might be drawn to inappropriately influence young receptive minds and engage in political polemics. However, the opposite is true. Instead, we seek to clarify how the current political landscape has affected and at times obscured the science of environmental studies.

In fact, all Jewish Studies courses that seek to influence the moral development of students should be seen in the same light as a civics or government class. While Social Studies teachers who are registered voters are probably tempted to teach about the American political party system in a way that will cast a more favorable light on their party of choice, most understand that such conduct is not professionally appropriate or even effective. However, all Social Studies teachers would probably agree that in order for their students to be responsible future voters, they must be educated about all sides of issues and be familiar with the political landscape of the country. Similarly, we argued that Jewish students, as potential political and moral leaders of the future, must be informed about issues of environmentalism and encouraged to define their own moral stands and regard them from a Jewish perspective. Teaching from a perspective of moral absolutism stifles debate and intellectual inquiry. Therefore, it is important that the study of the environment provide an opportunity to engage in moral introspection and ethical articulation in light of the Jewish tradition.

Another unique and morally relevant aspect of the course "Living on God's Earth" is that it is an integrated, interdisciplinary seminar in science, moral philosophy, economic theory, and Jewish text study. It is possible to teach environmental science, economics, sociology, Jewish texts, and environmental philosophers in greater depth if each subject is relegated to a separate course; however, each is insufficient without the other. The synergy of combining these subjects in a single course produces a web of natural connections among the ideas. For example, reading Garret Harden's seminal essay "The Tragedy of the Commons" enabled students to understand certain sections of the Talmud in a new light. Harden describes how the overuse of common resources leads to inevitable degradation of these resources for everyone. Even the use of one's own property can have unintended deleterious consequences on the public good. This concept can be applied to the following selection from *Baba Kama* 50b:

Our Rabbis taught: A man should not remove stones from his property and put them in the public property. Once there was a man who was throwing stones from his property into the public way. A pious man found him doing this and said, "You empty-headed fool, why are you clearing property which is not yours and putting the stones onto property which is yours?! Difficult days came upon the man and he had to sell his field. [One day] he was walking in the public path and stumbled over the very stones [which he had placed there]. He said, "What the pious man said was true, 'why are you clearing property which is not yours and putting the stones onto property which is yours?'"

This story is studied in order to question our concept of "private property" from a communal and moral perspective and how its use can affect the public domain. For instance, to apply the model of the "tragedy of the commons": if every farmer deposited the rocks from his fields in the public wayfares, it would severely disrupt travel, which would then also affect the farmers who helped to create this situation in the first place. This story can also be interpreted symbolically: the rocks can be understood as waste products that we vent into the atmosphere and dump into the rivers, the oceans, or empty lots. These represent the "commons" for all humanity. In this case, the ultimate consequences of these actions have already come back to haunt us in soil erosion, smog-filled cities, and the loss of habitat and biodiversity. This is just one example of how the integration of Jewish sources, environmental philosophy, and ecological understanding can produce powerful insights that would not happen if these subjects were studied separately.

Jewish educators have the opportunity to challenge students to develop a new set of morals and ethics that will govern the use of the land and the world's resources. Many educators, scientists, and politicians are realizing that a global reexamination and change of values is required. Perhaps only the inculcation of a new set of morals can have an effect that is sufficiently pervasive to affect humanity's impact on the environment now and in the future. However, such change happens slowly. Environmental education that deals explicitly with issues of moral valuation of nature's systems from a Jewish perspective can have a profound impact on how people think and behave. Jewish educators should be working to imbue all subjects, especially Jewish Studies, with morally relevant discussions and analyses.

MINYONIM

Prayer can provide a spiritual context for our lives; however, this doesn't always come naturally. Jewish children and teenagers need to be taught how to pray, why to pray, and ways to make Jewish prayer a significant part of their lives. Despite the best efforts, this will not always succeed; however, the potential results are well worth the effort. All formats of Jewish education should incorporate at least one daily Jewish worship service (a *minyon*) into their formal educational programs. Not only is prayer a vital aspect of the Jewish tradition, the discipline and skills required, as well as the concepts that make up Jewish prayer, are essential elements of effective Jewish education.

Prayer is a means of building self-discipline. Anyone who plays a musical instrument or participates intensively in a sport or engages in some other artistic pursuit is aware of how many hours of practice, drudgery, tedium, exercising, workouts, or rough sketches are necessary before he or she can achieve any measure of expertise or even enjoyment. For a pianist to perform in public and for an athlete to achieve greatness in a sports event, he or she must have devoted hours and hours to some kind of boring and frustrating practice, often passing up many everyday pleasures in order to train. Anything that is worthwhile doing in life and that gives us a rewarding experience takes effort, time, patience, continuity, and devotion.

How often have we heard Jews come into the synagogue on the High Holy Days or to a Bar or Bat Mitzvah service as guests and then either praise or criticize the rabbi or *hazzan* depending on whether they were given a "religious experience"? Experiencing a spiritual moment or feeling must be worked on as hard as any of the sports or skills that we try to master in other areas of life. Prayer is as much an art as it is a skill. Prayer demands as much time and attention (and often tedium) in order to achieve a moment of high religious inspiration as any other worthwhile endeavor. Jewish students should be encouraged to engage in this lifelong pursuit of spirituality by working on their prayer skills—not simply technical proficiency skills, but the ability to consistently devote time and energy to the preparation for spirituality. Scheduling daily prayer services can provide students with the opportunities to learn how to be receptive and work to achieve spirituality in their lives. Disciplining oneself to pray regularly is the only way to achieve the experience of emotionally fulfilling prayer.

Prayer is a means of linking individual Jews with the larger Jewish community, both geographically (around the world) and historically (through time). Although an individual Jew can pray alone, the Jewish tradition encourages Jews to pray together as a community—with a minimum of ten people to form a *minyon*. Rabbi Moses ben Maimon (Maimonides) wrote, "An individual should always try to join a congregation and not pray alone whenever he has the opportunity to pray with a congregation. . . . Whoever dwells in a community with a synagogue and doesn't pray there with the congregation, he is called a 'bad neighbor'" (*Mishneh Torah,* Laws of Prayer, 8:1).

In fact, the majority of all prayers in the prayer book are formulated in the plural. An individual can say the *Birkat HaMazon* (grace after meals) alone but the blessing is in plural; "*We* thank you, Lord our God,. . . for the land which you gave *us.*" Even the *Amidah* (standing prayer), the heart of every prayer service in which we silently address our thoughts to God, is formulated in the plural: "*We* thank you and acknowledge that you are *our* God and God of *our* ancestors." And on Yom Kippur, in the section entitled, Confession of Sins, each sentence begins: "For the sins that *we* have committed." (Italics added in the quotes above.)

In addition, although many religious rituals are performed individually, such as saying the blessing before putting on a *talit* (prayer shawl) or *tefillin* (phylacteries), taking the *lulav* (palm branch) and *etrog* (citron) on Sukkot, or lighting Shabbat candles, the prayers recited are all the same: that is, Jews who perform such actions around the world are all united through the recitation of similar prayers. Also, Jews who have recited such prayers throughout Jewish history, from Rabbinic times to the present day, have recited essentially the same prayers. The prayers that are recited on Shabbat morning in any given synagogue are essentially the same prayers that are being said by hundreds of thousands of Jews all over the world that morning. And these are also nearly the exact same prayers that have been recited by Jews for the past two thousand years. These *tefillot* (prayers) are a powerful means through which Jews can create connections between themselves and other Jews. In other words, prayer links us as individual Jews to the entire Jewish people, past and present.

Prayer is a way to engage in self-analysis. One of the basic goals of Jewish worship is to encourage us on a regular, daily basis to confront the essence of ourselves. The prayers lead us to ask ourselves who we are, what is important to us, how we relate to others, and what are our goals in life. One opinion in the Jewish tradition claims that one of the highest forms of prayer is silence. This pure contemplation is to be devoted to introspection and thoughts of God. Daily prayer, which reflects and embodies the values and insights of the Jewish tradition, provides the format for this continuous self-confrontation.

One of the tasks of prayer is to push us from where we are now—emotionally, intellectually, and interpersonally—to where we ought to be. But this self-analysis is more than simply, "getting in touch with yourself." The self-analysis involved in prayer demands that the worshipper confront the values and standards of the Jewish tradition as represented in the prayer book. Various prayers encourage the worshipper to thank God for their lives and for all of the bounty of this world, which has been provided for their sustenance. Other prayers encourage gratitude, reverence, a love of God, a desire to avoid untrustworthy companions, as well as requests for self-control, knowledge, the ability to forgive others, physical health and prosperity, and all of the manifold needs and hopes of most people. Just by reading the prayers, by comparing ourselves to the spiritual and ethical ideals laid down in the prayer book, we can begin to analyze our lives and who we are. Jewish students should be encouraged to engage in this self-reflective process through prayer in order to develop thoughtful and deliberate growth and maturation.

Prayer is a natural response to being alive. Perhaps the real challenge of prayer is to retain an almost childish sense of wonder and awe at the incredible experience of being alive. Anyone who has seen the wonder on a baby's face when he or she sees an airplane, a dog, or a butterfly knows what this reaction to life includes. All of us, at one time or another, have felt an overwhelming feeling of amazement while witnessing a spectacular natural phenomenon, such as seeing snow-capped peaks in the distance or watching a storm come in. Perhaps we have felt moved when having a wonderful experience with good friends, or suddenly been struck by profound ideas in a book or movie. Prayer is the natural human response to these experiences.

Have you have ever climbed a mountain or a hill? Have you ever been dazzled by the beauty of the view that you saw? It is relatively easy to express our feelings of being overwhelmed and describe the sight to a friend immediately afterwards. But it is not so simple to remember how you felt, or describe what you saw, even just a few days later, let alone in a month or a year. It is natural to forget the emotional intensity of such experiences with the passage of time. We enjoy them when they happen, but it is difficult to hold on to such emotions as awe and wonder.

We can't always return to the mountain top when we want or need an intense spiritual feeling. However, prayer can help us to recreate that sense of awe and wonder. The ideas expressed in our prayers challenge us to look at life around us with fresh, new eyes. One line in the morning prayers speaks of God as "renewing in goodness, every day and continually, the work of creation." The prayers challenge us to see that which is familiar as new, interesting, and full of wonder. It doesn't always work, but, sometimes, prayer can help us remember what we felt when we stood at the top of that mountain. Jewish students should be encouraged to strive to recreate this sense of awe and wonder in their everyday lives through prayer.

Prayer helps to regulate each day. We all have our own daily rituals. I walk my dog early every morning and say hello to the same people walking their own dogs. This ritual not only helps my dog, but it helps me to wake up and consider what I need to do that day. Daily prayer can help regulate our days by providing us with a moment or two of spiritual reassurance. It reminds us that we are spiritual creatures, not only on Shabbat and holidays or Rosh HaShanah and Yom Kippur, but every day.

Daily prayer provides a structure with which to experience our days. The *Shaharit* (morning) service enables us to formulate the coming day in spiritual terms: how do we want to approach this day? How do we want to greet our friends and family and face the daily challenges? *Minha* (the afternoon service) provides a spiritual oasis in the middle or toward the end of a day in which to check ourselves: Have we been following through on the plans that we set in the morning? Do we need to regain a more spiritual perspective of our day? For students in a setting of formal Jewish education, davening *Shaharit* and/or *Minha* can be powerful means of bringing a sense of God's presence into the most mundane of days by creating a spiritual structure for experiencing each day.

Prayer is a mitzvah. The Hebrew word *mitzvah* is commonly thought to mean "a good deed." However, the actual translation of the word is "commandment." Prayer is understood by the Jewish tradition as an obligation incumbent upon all Jews to engage in three times a day. Prayer is not always an activity that people want to do; after all, it can become repetitive and boring. Sometimes it can even feel like a burden or a chore. However, the analogy with prayer as a chore can be instructive. Chores are often performed out of a sense of obligation: that is, if I don't take out the garbage, no one else will. We also do chores out of the sense of obligation that comes from being involved in a loving relationship. As children, we performed household chores not because we enjoyed them but because we felt obligated to do what our parents asked. We loved our parents enough to be willing to do tasks that we didn't like, understanding that this was part of what it meant to be involved in a loving relationship. Similarly, prayer is a "chore" in that it is an obligation in the Jewish tradition that devolves upon all Jews because we understand ourselves to be involved in an ongoing, loving relationship with God. All *mitzvot,* that is, commandments, are obligations that Jews are supposed to fulfill out of a sense of love— love of God and God's love for us. By praying, we demonstrate and reinforce this love every day.

Prayer is a form of Torah study. The study of the Torah is an important part of what it means to be a Jew. Every day, Jews are obligated to make time to study some part of our tradition in order to learn more about Judaism and the Torah. Because not everyone has the time to study Torah or Talmud every day, many passages from the Bible and Rabbinic literature are incorporated into the prayer book, thus giving every Jew the opportunity to study a little Torah. Many prayers contain quotes from the Bible and the Talmud, so simply reciting the prayers in the prayer book is an act of studying Judaism. For instance the main paragraphs of the *Shema* are selections from the Torah. The first part of the *Shema*, "Hear O Israel, the Lord is our God, the Lord is one," comes from the book of Deuteronomy (6:4), as does the paragraph after it. The paragraph that commands us to wear *tzitzit* (fringes) on our *talitot* comes from the book of Numbers in the Torah. Nearly all of the blessings and passages that we recite in the *Amidah* on a weekday, Shabbat, or holiday, come from the Talmud. Plus, the many Psalms that we recite as part of our services, such as the Ashrei, come from the book of *Tehilim* (Psalms) in the Bible. In short, whenever we pray using our Siddur, we are reciting large portions of Biblical books and Rabbinic works.

The Jewish tradition maintains that studying Torah is another way of worshipping God, whether we do it while praying or actually sitting down to read the Bible and other selections from Rabbinic literature. Reading passages from the Bible or the Talmud is understood as studying a message that God has conveyed to the Jewish people. Continual reexamination of these messages can yield further, deeper insights and knowledge. Jewish students should be encouraged to encounter God and the wisdom of the Jewish tradition in all contexts of Jewish life, especially Jewish prayer.

Prayer encourages spirituality and connection to God. Prayer is about communing with God. However students may conceive of God, establishing a daily or regular prayer service within a format of Jewish education communicates the message that Jewish learning is intimately connected with learning how to relate to God. In an age in which many people feel a distinct lack of spirituality in their lives and feel alienated from God's presence, perhaps one of the most important experiences that Jewish educators can share with and help to build within their students is a feeling of spiritual adequacy and the opportunity to relate to God on a daily basis. Whether students like or dislike prayer, it is important for young Jews to confront this traditional format for experiencing God's presence or attempting to find it within themselves.

For all of these reasons, all formats of Jewish education should incorporate at least one daily Jewish worship service into their formal educational programs.

MISHMAROT

In my school, students run their own *minyonim* (daily prayer services). If such responsibility had been thrust upon them with no plan or structure, it is unlikely that this experiment would have succeeded. Therefore, they were provided with a structure and means to share this responsibility. Our student-run *minyons* have been overwhelmingly successful. Here is how we created a *minyon* run and organized by students and why.

The problem. First, an anecdote: I once saw a young man, a recent Bar Mitzvah, not wearing his *talit* during Shabbat morning services in my own synagogue. Having attended his Bar Mitzvah, I recalled the pride that this young man had proclaimed in his Jewish heritage and the excitement that he had expressed in his new responsibilities vis-à-vis worship services. His beautiful *talit* was a prominent new addition to his usual Shabbat attire on the occasion of his Bar Mitzvah. Seeing him some weeks later without his *talit* during services, I asked him why he no longer wore his *talit*? He told me that prayer was not "cool" at the Jewish day school that he attended and that to show any evidence of interest in prayer was to call unwanted negative attention to one's self. He explained that this attitude had "worn off" on him and that he was now unable to take an interest in prayer as a result of his negative prayer experiences at school even though he had recently graduated from there.

An entirely subjective and anecdotal survey of many day schools' daily morning worship services indicates to me that many such *minyonim* are failing to excite students about Jewish prayer or to inculcate in Jewish children any desire to participate voluntarily in or increase their knowledge about *tefillot.* That some students do graduate from our day schools as knowledgeable, *davening* (praying) young Jews is unfortunately the exception that proves the rule. In my personal encounters with a large number of Jewish children in day schools and young adult alumni of such schools, I have been saddened to discover profound apathy, if not actual hostility, to Jewish prayer in a communal setting. Such apathy and hostility represent a formidable challenge for American synagogues and congregational rabbis. Are we hurting both the spiritual lives of our children and our communal organizations in the very attempt to strengthen them? It doesn't have to be this way.

My own childhood experiences, I fear, are not unique. Despite my years of Hebrew School attendance, Bar Mitzvah training, Temple confirmation, and enforced attendance of years of High Holiday services, I was still almost completely ignorant of the most basic core of Jewish prayers, not to mention the Hebrew language itself. As a college student unfamiliar with Jewish prayer, I found learning to lead the prayers myself and organize *minyonim* to be a tremendously empowering experience significant to my development as a Jew. What changed for me was being personally challenged to create a Jewish prayer experience that I, myself, would want to attend. Only then was I sufficiently intrigued to devote the necessary time and energy to mastering the pronunciation of the unfamiliar Hebrew words and memorizing the deeply resonant signature melodies of the Shabbat and weekday prayer services. When I was offered the opportunity to help create a new student *minyon* for the Solomon Schechter High School of Long Island, I decided to put my own personal experience to the test. Could this school create a *minyon* structure that would stimulate the students to take charge and make it their own?

My hope especially was to avoid duplicating several negative aspects of prayer services of Jewish day schools where teachers must cajole students into leading the services and plead or threaten other students in an effort to get them to read daily Torah readings. I have also seen teachers "patrol" the services by wandering up and down the aisles of the school synagogue space on the lookout for misbehavior and talking, disciplining students for whispering and acting inappropriately, and then, themselves, talking with fellow faculty members while ignoring the very services they are supposed to oversee. I viewed my challenge as creating a *minyon* that would be meaningful to both students and faculty.

The solution. From the outset, I believed that to achieve these goals the daily prayer services would have to be student-run. "Empowerment" is a much overused term, but it effectively describes the situation that I wanted to create. Empowering the students meant that they had to have an integral role and share of responsibility in running the services. Because my own school was brand new, I had no history to overcome. On the other hand, there were no traditions upon which to rely or fall back. Therefore, I faced both distinct advantages and disadvantages in trying to create a new, empowering student-run *minyon*.

Rather than create something new and untried, we actually brought back to life a very ancient institution: the *Mishmeret,* or "duty period." When the Second Temple still stood, a *Mishmeret* used to consist of a designated number of *Kohanim,* or priests, who would perform their appointed tasks in the Temple in Jerusalem in two-week "shifts." The *Kohanim* attended to the details of running an institution dedicated to animal sacrifices. In modern Judaism, prayer has replaced animal sacrifices; however, we adopted this concept, terminology, and the time-frame of the *Mishmeret* for the daily *minyon* and created a system of biweekly student *Mishmarot* to organize and run the daily *minyon*.

Before school began, I specifically asked two of the new incoming students, who I knew had experience in praying and reading Torah, to "volunteer" to be the first *Mishmeret*. I briefly outlined their duties and asked them for their reactions. They were extremely excited and flattered by their first assignment and accepted the role of the first *Mishmeret* with enthusiasm. During the first few days of school, I placed a calendar and sign-up list inside our *Beit Midrash* (place of study and prayer). Students chose a partner and a particular two-week period during which they assumed all responsibility for running the *minyon*.

I decided to clarify and formalize the responsibilities of the *Mishmeret* in advance in order to establish as quickly as possible an efficient system of breaking down the duties into manageable units. My concern was that students might feel overwhelmed with an undifferentiated mandate simply to "run the services" on their own. These responsibilities were clearly itemized as follows:

Service Leading: Finding fellow students to lead morning services each day of their two-week term. The *Mishmeret* could divide the service into *Birkot HaShahar* ("Morning Blessings," the initial, introductory prayers), *Pesukei DeZimra* ("Verses of Song," a selections of Psalms and Biblical verses preceding the main service), and *Shaharit* ("Dawn," the core of the daily morning service, consisting of the *Shema* and *Amidah*) so that one student would not be overwhelmed by doing everything alone.

Torah Reading: Finding fellow students to chant the weekly Torah reading on Mondays and Thursdays. Thus, the *Mishmeret* had to prepare enough in advance so that the Torah readers would have time to prepare their Torah readings. In addition, the *Mishmeret* had the option of serving themselves as *Gabbaim* (Torah service helpers) during the Torah service or finding other students to fill this role as well.

Synagogue Honors: Distributing honors during the service, such as *Aliyot* (being called up to the Torah), *P'tihot* (opening the Ark doors), and *Hagbah* and *G'lilah* (raising and wrapping the Torah).

D'var Torah: Finding one student each week to deliver a brief *D'var Torah* (explanation of the Biblical reading) on the weekly Torah portion.

Page Announcement: To stand on either side of the Reader's Table and announce all page numbers for the rest of the *minyon*.

Physical Set-Up: Ensuring that the Torah was rolled to the correct portion before each new reading, arranging the chairs in the *Beit Midrash* each morning as well as setting up the *Siddurim* (prayerbooks) for easy distribution each morning.

These were the basic tasks of the *Mishmeret*. If any student had trouble or questions either with the duties of the *Mishmeret* or with any part they volunteered for, they were directed to speak with me, for I was the faculty member designated as the *minyon* coordinator.

Jewish day schools should be committed to mandatory, daily morning services for their pupils as a matter of religious principle and obligation. Thus, when the institution of student *Mishmarot* was first presented to the students, no one had the option of refusing to serve on at least one *Mishmeret* that year. Those students who acted quickly and decisively were able to select their own partners and choose the two-week period of responsibility that they preferred. Those students who sought to avoid this responsibility did not have these choices: their partners were selected for them and they were assigned a two-week period of responsibility at random.

I believe the immediate institution of the *Mishmeret* system was especially effective because it focused discussion on responsibility for organizing and leading daily services rather than on the institution of mandatory prayer. Whether to have such prayers or not is moot because the institution of daily prayer is a required norm of religious behavior in the Jewish tradition. Communal prayer also provides the basis by which most American Jews participate in communal Jewish life. Therefore, any discussion about the value or fairness of mandatory daily prayer should be irrelevant in a day school setting. How to organize such prayers and how such responsibility will be shared among the students is a much more educational and productive topic of debate.

In addition, the institution of the *Mishmeret* system immediately challenged our students. Rather than create a polarization between students (who may or may not want to pray every morning), and faculty members (who have the responsibility for ensuring that students do, in fact, pray every morning), the *Mishmeret* system placed the burden of responsibility on the students. There was no opportunity to protest the validity of mandatory daily prayer. The students were given the much more productive challenge of having to organize these worship services as soon as possible. Those who accepted the challenge immediately were positively reinforced by having their pick of partners and time slots. Thus, the *Mishmeret* system created an opportunity to positively reinforce such skills as timely planning and the channeling of energy into productive and constructive avenues of activity.

The results. The first and most obvious overall effect of the *Mishmeret* system was the consistently well organized and familiar nature of daily worship services. Everyone knew his or her role in advance. Students who led services arrived early in order to begin on time, Torah readers prepared in advance, and the students of each *Mishmeret* kept all of the diverse elements necessary for a positive davening experience running smoothly. Despite the fact that some students took their *Mishmeret* responsibilities less seriously than others—and as a result services were sometimes a little confused—overall, the daily *minyon* functioned more efficiently and flawlessly than either faculty or students could have anticipated.

Perhaps the most important result of the *Mishmeret* system was the general atmosphere of the daily *minyon*. In stark contrast to *minyonim* in other Jewish day schools, our daily *minyon* became a time and place for true quiet contemplation and prayer. Even with the inevitable presence of inveterate chatterers inherent in any student body, the *minyon* was characterized by calm and quiet, broken—or perhaps enhanced—only by those who were accustomed to pronouncing their private prayers audibly. A seemingly genuine feeling of respect and sanctity pervaded our *Beit Midrash* each morning. The occasional intrusion of giggles and laughter that accompanied any mishap or minor discipline problem only served to underscore the fact that a respectful calm and quiet was the norm.

So natural and powerful was this atmosphere of concentration and *kavanah* (focus, intensity) that visiting schools and classes that joined our *minyon* commented on what they perceived to be the unusually and extraordinarily calm nature of our services. During one visit of an eighth grade class, a number of the visiting students openly expressed their amazement about the atmosphere of the *minyon*. When a seventh grade class joined us for a *Rosh Hodesh* (new moon) *minyon,* some of these visiting students later remarked to me, "It's so different from our services! Everyone really *davens* (prays) in the high school!" Whether true or not, the perception this comment communicates is of significance. Even our own students, who were not always completely aware of the uniqueness of our *minyon,* after we joined another school's worship services, pleaded not to participate in other worship services again. They hadn't appreciated what they, themselves, had created until they had been confronted with an alternative!

When we instituted the *Mishmeret* system, we hoped that, as the students realized that they were creating a *minyon* for themselves, they would feel more enthusiastic about expanding their own participation. We found that this did happen and attribute it to the following: First, as each *Mishmeret* became aware of those students who possessed strong davening and Torah-reading skills, they sought out those students again and again. However, as expected, even those students who enjoyed leading *tefillot* and reading Torah began to tire of doing it so often, and therefore, began to refuse the requests of the *Mishmeret*. Thus rebuffed, the *Mishmarot* were left with no recourse but to try to encourage those students less sure of themselves to participate in the *minyon* more actively. As a result of such positive and encouraging peer pressure, more and more students began to try their own hand at leading the *tefillot* and reading Torah. The division of the daily morning service into several parts proved instrumental in encouraging these students to become more active.

The second reason for broader involvement in the *minyon* is that students felt safe to experiment and assume greater public roles. Many students brushed up on prayer-leading skills and some even paired up with friends and learned an entirely new synagogue skill. By the end of the first year, absolutely every student in the ninth grade had participated in some way, no matter how small, in organizing and running our *minyon*. This pattern has continued with extremely high levels of student participation in daily services.

In order to reinforce the seriousness of the *minyon*, I scheduled private conferences with each student to discuss his or her feelings about the *minyon*, his or her own role in it, and how the student could continue to be challenged spiritually. Despite the fact that the *minyon* was not a class and that students did not receive a grade, the daily morning services were, nonetheless, a vital part of our informal Jewish education. Therefore, it was important that students take their role in the *minyon* seriously. By and large, the majority of students did express satisfaction and even excitement with the *minyon*. Many confided that they had never experienced such an open and inviting prayer experience. Indeed, many students voluntarily shared their goals for the next year, be it learning a new synagogue skill, how to read Torah, or simply to volunteer to receive more *Aliyot* on Torah-reading days. My overwhelming impression from these conferences was how successful the creation of a new type of *minyon* had been and continues to be.

To highlight the importance of *minyon*, students were informed that a brief, neutral, descriptive set of observations from several faculty members concerning their behavior in *minyon* would become a permanent part of their nonacademic record at the end of each year. While clearly such an observation can in no way comment on the internal, subjective quality of each student's experience in the *minyon*, student behavior, such as apparent attentiveness and level of participation, was deemed a legitimate matter of interest for the school to document. Rather than focus on the potentially negative aspects of such an observation, we emphasized the value of such observations in tracking a student's religious growth and development. As a religious school committed to the spiritual growth and development of students, it was important to take their religious growth and involvement in *minyon* seriously.

Unexpected positive results. Some additional positive outcomes of the creation of a student-run *minyon* were that it led to increased student-initiated innovations and improvements in the *minyon,* encouraged the positive use of these *minyon*-based public responsibilities, and encouraged students to apply the *Mishmeret* model to other, altogether different areas of student life. One of the innovations that the institution of the *Mishmeret* encouraged was the creation of a *Minha* (afternoon) service each day for all interested students. Everyone was welcome to come and participate, and whatever students were present simply organized the responsibilities of running the prayer service on the spot.

Another positive result of the creation of public roles of responsibilities was the use of weekly *Divrei Torah* (teaching or lesson) for positive, school-related "political" purposes. Towards the end of the year, several students ingeniously took advantage of the *D'var Torah* by using it as a soap-box cleverly to argue the validity of their positions before their peers and faculty, regardless of the connection to the weekly Torah portion. For example, students spoke about the unfairness of summer assignments or the format of student government as being inherent in the weekly Torah portion. Regardless of the issue, students awoke to the possibilities of the constructive use of public roles of responsibility.

A final indication that the *Mishmeret* system was a success was the application of this model to other areas of student life in our school. When it became clear that some students were not living up to their responsibility to keep the Student Center and hallways free of trash and debris, the subject of cleanliness became a much-debated topic at our weekly Town Hall meetings. While some students assumed occasional responsibility for cleaning up after their peers, they had no intention of taking on the additional role of garbage collector permanently. In the midst of this debate, a number of students raised the idea of the creation of a "*Mishmeret Nikiyon*," or a "cleanliness" duty roster. Although this suggestion was never implemented, it demonstrated that even the students clearly saw the *Mishmeret* system as an example of how successfully to share the burden of communal responsibilities.

Conclusion. Our experiment in creating a student-run *minyon* was a success. The institution of the *Mishmeret* system succeeded in empowering our students to assume responsibility for their own daily morning worship services. The daily *minyon* flourished and has been recognized as a major element in the success of our school. A final piece of evidence reveals the ultimate success of this model, and this concerns the role of faculty in the daily morning *minyon*.

While I served as the *Minyon* Coordinator, my actual, daily responsibilities in the day-to-day running of the *minyon* were negligible. I gave frequent short lessons throughout the year during the prayer services to teach the students about such subjects as the choreography of Jewish prayer, the significance of different passages, the structure of the morning service, and various philosophical reasons for why Jews should pray. Similarly, whereas all faculty members were required to attend daily morning *minyon,* no one faculty member played any more of a particular role than another. The one role that was shared equally was trying to instill a minimum level of respect by occasionally quietly asking a student to refrain from chatting with a neighbor or perhaps casting an arch expression across the room towards a student who appeared more interested in making faces at a friend than in following along in the *Siddur.*

However, what was significant was that the *Beit Midrash* was transformed into a space where teenagers and adults could daven together and make a spiritual home together. There was a shared sense of spiritual cooperation among everyone involved. Adolescents and adults alike took a daily prayer service in a Jewish day school and transformed it into a model for true community.

HESHBON NEFESH AND CONTINUOUS LEARNING

Heshbon Nefesh literally means "taking stock of one's soul." It is an activity or process that the Jewish tradition assigns as preparation for the high holy days of *Rosh HaShanah* and *Yom Kippur*. Individual Jews are supposed to look inside themselves and determine what they did wrong in the previous year and how they can improve themselves in the coming year. In the world of Jewish education, teachers must be engaged in a continuous process of *heshbon nefesh* in which they reevaluate their teaching style, methods, and classroom activities. When previously successful lesson plans begin to go "stale" or fail, it is time for teachers to return to the drawing board and generate new tactics and approaches. Even when lessons don't fail, all educators must continue to challenge themselves by tackling new material. Although no teacher enjoys creating new lessons and activities to replace old, familiar ones, this process is essential, and often inescapable, in order to respond to the changing needs of new generations of students. And the most important component in renewing curricula is teacher renewal—not changing teachers, but ensuring that the teachers are renewed in their work and commitment to teaching and learning.

It is not possible for motivational speakers to motivate others unless they, themselves, are motivated people. Similarly, it is difficult for teachers to communicate excitement about learning unless they are excited about learning themselves. In order for teachers to be able to communicate excitement about learning, it is imperative that educators continue to experience this same excitement by continuing their own studies. Jewish educators, whether they actually teach Jewish Studies or not, should invest their time in studying Jewish texts for their own personal spiritual and intellectual enrichment.

Many teachers are reluctant to do this, however, for a number of reasons. The first is lack of time. If educators aren't provided enough time to prepare their own lessons and grade papers, how can they possibly be expected to invest whatever time remains to their own regular studies?

Also, many educators long ago have stopped studying for the sake of learning and their own spiritual and intellectual stimulation and, instead, devote their time to studying as a means of preparation of their lesson plans. This kind of study, however, often lacks joy and enthusiasm because it is study for the sake of work. Although teaching a class year after year builds teacher confidence and expertise, it leaves little incentive to seek out and study new materials if they are not to be taught or somehow included in lesson plans.

With whom should teachers study? As teachers already spend a great deal of time with other faculty members during each school day, is it realistic to expect them to study with one another? Is it possible to glean new insights and find inspiration among the familiar faces of colleagues? And, given the lack of time (and money), how can other experts and scholars be enticed to help teachers continue their own studies?

While school administrators, principals, and board members are dedicated to the educational excellence of the students, they must also be dedicated to the ongoing, continuous education and professional growth of teachers. If teachers don't grow and learn, they can become bored, stale, and stuck. To communicate the real joy and excitement of learning to students, teachers need to be engaged in this process themselves.

If a school doesn't provide the time or opportunity, teachers must make the time on their own to study. This is not a question of allocating precious time but one of priorities. Educators must be encouraged to make the time for personal study and to recognize the value of studying topics that are not directly related to their curricula. Learning texts and subjects other than those he or she teaches can help broaden a teacher's perspective and depth of knowledge in general. It can also enable a teacher to rediscover the joy of learning for its own sake.

In addition, teachers in a department should be encouraged to study together. Members of a *havruta* (study group) learn from each other, sharing insights and knowledge and supporting one another in their mutual quest to continue their education. Studying with fellow faculty members can help strengthen the communal bonds of teachers, which can improve the sense of community in the whole school. In-service professional growth days should not be solely dedicated to professionally relevant subjects of entirely practical use to teachers. These days should be faculty learning days, when all of the teachers of a school are given the opportunity to study Torah and Jewish texts with guest teachers, scholars, and rabbis in the community. The excitement that such programs generate can motivate an entire faculty and provide additional community-building experiences.

For teachers to motivate others, they must devote the time and energy to motivate themselves and have the opportunity to be motivated by others. Faculty members are not the final word in education; rather, they are links in a vast chain of learning. And in order for this chain to be lengthy and strong, Jewish educators must do everything they can to strengthen their own links before they can even begin to attend to the issue of adding new links to the chain.

Part Three

JEWISH STUDIES CURRICULA

THE GREAT POTENTIAL OF JEWISH EDUCATION

Although there is a consensus that Jewish education is part of the solution to the problem of alienation, assimilation, and intermarriage in the American Jewish community, there is no consensus as to what this Jewish education should consist of. The Hebrew word *bekiut* literally means "expertise," but what expertise should Jewish students develop? And given the fact that there is not, nor will ever be, sufficient time to cover everything that probably should be covered in Jewish Studies classes, which topics should take precedence? Should students learn how to perform and observe practical religious rituals, or should they learn Bible, *Mishnah, Gemara, Midrash,* or Jewish History? And which texts and topics should be covered?

As important as Jewish education is in the elementary and middle school years, it is crucial in the high school years. Despite the best and most intensive efforts to convey significant Jewish values and ritual and ethical practices to students during the middle school years, or even in elementary school, teenagers are developmentally better prepared to learn and absorb Jewish learning in greater depth and sophistication. Therefore, whatever Jewish teens are taught during these years should be designed or chosen to have the maximum impact possible on their intellectual and spiritual development.

Whatever consensus might exist regarding the future of Jewish youth, it is clear that many educators want to ensure that young Jews will not be alienated from their religion or people. Therefore, teens should be sufficiently educated about Jewish life, history, religious practice, philosophy, and literature to feel a part of the Jewish people. Jewish teens should also be Jewishly educated so that they are less likely to assimilate into the general population, giving up any claim to their Jewish identity. They should be taught positive reasons for being Jewish and given opportunities to enjoy Jewish experiences that will connect them emotionally to Judaism and the Jewish people. They should learn why Jews are a distinct people and why their religion is unique. And, finally, Jewish teens should be given an education that will positively impact on their decision as to whom to marry when that time in their life arrives. Their education should be such that they will want to build a Jewish life with their spouses, who will share the same moral, ethical, spiritual, and religious values.

However, these goals of wanting to educate young Jews so that they will not be alienated from Judaism, won't assimilate, and won't intermarry, are negative reasons. They ignore the great potential of Jewish education to achieve far greater and more positive goals. Speaking of negative goals, I once had a conversation with a fellow Jewish educator about the ultimate goals of Jewish education in which she confided to me that her highest educational goal was to create future "Jewish mothers and fathers." She looked upon every Jewish child she taught from this point of view and based her entire educational philosophy and curricular choices on what type of Jewish parents she wanted her students to become. In other words, she focused on the impression of Judaism and Jewish knowledge these future Jewish mothers and fathers would ultimately pass on to their children.

Viewing Jewish students of all ages as merely "future Jewish mothers and fathers"—no matter the Jewish educational setting—subtly communicates a number of negative educational messages to the students and also ignores the incredible potential of Jewish education. The first negative message that this goal subtly communicates is that Jews as individuals are irrelevant except as messengers of the Jewish tradition to their future children. By viewing Jewish students—at best—as merely future Jewish mothers and fathers is to denigrate the value of their future accomplishments in life. Perhaps these young Jews will one day become great academics, accomplished artists, professionals, scientists, engineers, successful business people, or extraordinarily compassionate and giving men and women in addition to becoming parents. Should the goal of their Jewish education be to denigrate their vast potential as human beings and view them as merely future Jewish mothers and fathers? Perhaps such gifted, talented, and successful Jewish men and women will, indeed, become mothers and fathers and will, in fact, create rich, fulfilling Jewish home environments for their children. But to view all Jewish students as merely future

Jewish mothers and fathers is to convey the subconscious message that the individual worth and intellectual, spiritual, or professional accomplishments of these children is irrelevant or, at best, is of secondary value.

Another negative message that this goal communicates is that Jews can only be fulfilled as Jews by becoming parents. While the goal of propagation is, indeed, very highly valued in the Jewish tradition—for the very first commandment of the Torah is to be "fruitful and multiply" (Genesis 1:28)—to make this the highest goal of Jewish education is not without risk. First of all, a Jewish education that values Jews only in their role as potential parents will only increase the guilt, frustration, and desperation that infertile couples already face. Infertility is a sufficient burden for couples struggling to achieve conception without adding a helping of Jewish guilt. It is unconscionable to suggest to infertile Jewish couples that their inability to have children limits their ability to fulfill themselves as Jews. Secondly, in an age when increasingly more and more advanced education is required to function in any given profession, the pursuit of higher degrees is a necessary component for economic survival. Such higher education can, and frequently does, delay the raising of a family. Jewish education that stresses only future parenthood risks increasing the emotional stress of Jewish adults as they pursue their education into their peak childrearing years. Balancing a career with the desire to begin a family is a difficult struggle for many people. Jewish educators should not add to the difficulty of these choices by overemphasizing the importance of raising Jewish children.

In addition, some Jews may choose not to raise children or even not to marry. While such a choice is clearly not desirable from the standpoint of the Jewish tradition—especially in a post-Holocaust world concerned with Jewish demographics—emphasizing parenthood as the ultimate goal of Jewish education risks alienating these Jews from our community. And, finally, no matter what position Jews and Jewish educators may take on homosexuality and lesbianism, even the most stringent reading of relevant sources demands the acceptance of such Jews into the Jewish community regardless of whether segments of the Jewish community cannot condone their sexual activities. Emphasizing parenthood as the ultimate goal of Jewish education risks further alienating these Jews as well as further complicating their own search for Jewish identity.

Still another negative message this goal communicates is that the ultimate purpose of Jewish education is "Jewish continuity." While the larger American Jewish community may currently be obsessed with assimilation, alienation, and intermarriage, and while Jewish education has the potential to positively affect such modern sociological phenomena and reverse such trends, the ultimate goal of Jewish education is not merely to serve as an antidote to this problem. To view all Jewish students as merely future Jewish mothers and fathers further fans the flames of the current hysteria about Jewish continuity. Jewish continuity is not the be-all and end-all of the Jewish tradition. Mere demographic national survival is not the goal of Jewish education. Therefore, emphasizing parenthood as the ultimate goal of Jewish education further politicizes and dilutes the spiritual intensity of Jewish education and reduces it to a mere solution to a problem.

And, finally, viewing Jewish students as merely future Jewish mothers and fathers ignores the incredible potential of Jewish education and ensures that the highest level of Jewish education ever attempted will always be at a simplistic, practical level. The creation of Jewish curricula that is intended only so that the recipients will one day be able to create a Jewish home environment will never rise above the level of associating *Rosh HaShanah* with apples and honey and *Yom Kippur* with saying "I'm sorry." Such an educational goal appeals to the lowest possible common denominator of Jewish—or perhaps human—existence, namely, procreation. Viewing all students as merely future Jewish mothers and fathers wastes the vast potential of Jewish education and indicates a profound lack of vision.

The goals of Jewish education should be much broader and vastly more ambitious. The primary goal of Jewish education should be radically to transform the lives of any and all Jews who come into contact with the Jewish tradition. Jewish educators should strive to challenge young Jews to be lifelong learners about and practitioners of the Jewish religion. One of the most important ways that Jewish education can potentially achieve these goals is to establish a sense of God's presence through the study of Jewish texts and the observance of Jewish rituals. Jewish education should serve to awaken and strengthen the spiritual life of Jews and bring them to an awareness of the potential of God's presence in their lives.

In order to radically transform the lives of Jews through Jewish education, educators should work to engage Jews emotionally and intellectually on the highest levels possible. One way to achieve this goal is to study Jewish texts using all of the traditional sources as well as the modern scholarly critical tools available today. Studying traditional Jewish texts such as the Bible, *Mishnah, Gemara,* and *Midrash* along with traditional commentaries has the potential to open students' eyes to the strong emotional currents present in our traditional texts. Anyone who reads the narratives about King David, the prophetic denunciations of Jeremiah, and the intensely personal laments contained in the book of Psalms cannot fail to be moved by the emotional intensity of the sacred texts. Delving into the complicated arguments of the *Mishnah* and *Gemara* and trying to decipher the cryptic imaginative twists and turns of Rabbinic Aggadic speculation can challenge even the most motivated and committed students of Rabbinic literature. Studying these very same texts using modern critical methodologies can open up entire new vistas on the personalities of the Biblical and Rabbinic characters and the psychological struggles that animated them. Jewish education should seek to excite Jews and encourage them to become personally involved in trying to reinterpret our ancient texts in order to make them relevant for our generation.

Another way to radically transform the lives of Jews through Jewish education is to provide all Jews, young and old, male and female, Hebrew literate or not, with the skills necessary to participate in our ongoing tradition. Jewish children and adults, singles and parents, all should be taught not only about Jewish holidays, *Shabbat, Kashrut,* and *Tefillah,* but also how to celebrate the Jewish holidays, observe *Shabbat* and *Kashrut,* and how to pray from a highly spiritual and sophisticated point of view. Such knowledge and skills should be taught not merely as tidbits to be passed along to the next generation, but for the spiritual and practical enjoyment and improvement of the learners themselves. The point of Jewish education is not how much Judaism students can pass along to their children, but how much Judaism can they themselves enjoy and benefit from emotionally, intellectually, and spiritually. In order to achieve and even surpass the goal of creating adequate future Jewish mothers and fathers, young Jews can, and should, be taught how to be passionate Jews themselves. If Jewish educators can impassion young Jews, they will create knowledgeable, committed, and dedicated Jewish parents of the future.

Instead of viewing Jewish education as a mere commodity to be passed along or as an antidote to a specific problem, such as the challenge of Jewish continuity, Jewish educators should be setting their sights much higher. Now is the time to raise the standards and expand the vision of the future of Jewish education. A precious opportunity is being wasted if the only vision educators have for Jewish students is that they will only become future Jewish parents. Rather, educators should look upon Jewish students as potential Jewish scholars and dedicated lay people as well as committed, Jewishly knowledgeable leaders of and participants in the Jewish community. All who educate and encourage even one Jewish student—it is as if they had educated and opened an entirely new, exciting, and challenging world of Jewish living and learning before them (based on *Mishnah Sanhedrin* 4:5).

THE RELIGION OF THE RABBIS

"How come we don't have sacrifices anymore if the Bible says that this is how we are supposed to worship God?" This and variations on this theme are the most common questions that Jewish Studies teachers are asked. The underlying feature of all such questions is that students assume that whatever is written in the Bible is what Jews should be doing in their religious life today. In fact, the majority of questions asked about Judaism by fellow Jews and gentiles alike stems from the common misunderstanding that modern Judaism is identical to the religion of the Bible.

In all fairness, this misunderstanding is actually quite logical. After all, most Jews know that religious Jews read from the Torah in synagogue on *Shabbat* and holidays. *Bar* and *Bat Mitzvah* students struggle for years or months to prepare to chant their Torah portions. Bible study classes are regular features of many synagogue Hebrew school curricula as well as adult education programs. It makes sense that most Jews draw the conclusion that the Torah is the holiest sacred book in the Jewish tradition. And the confusing thing is that they are not wrong! The Torah *is* the holiest book in the Jewish tradition, but the Torah is only the first sacred text in a long series of holy books that define the Jewish religion as it is practiced today. Jewish educators must take this fact into account as they create curricula and teach their classes. In order for modern Jews to understand their connections to the past and their place in the present, Jewish educators in all formats must incorporate information and texts that teach students where they fit into the progression of Jewish history—specifically, the difference between Biblical religion, the religion described in the Torah, and modern, that is, Rabbinic, Judaism.

Jews today are not Biblical Jews: they are Rabbinic Jews. Once, nearly two thousand years ago, Jews used to bring animal sacrifices to the Temple, the symbolic dwelling place of God's presence on earth, which was located in Jerusalem. There, a hierarchy of priests and levitical Temple workers attended to the complex and demanding rituals of animal sacrifices. Back then, Jews understood the direct connection between their religious rituals and what was written in the Torah. The religion that they practiced was nearly identical with what was described in the Torah. Such was the state of affairs for nearly one thousand years, with some disruptions due to wars and exile, until the Great Revolt of the Jews against the Roman empire in the years 66 C.E. (Common Era) to 70 C.E.

The level of disruption that this Jewish revolt caused the Romans, not to mention the embarrassment and anger it aroused due to the fact that the Jews initially won their first military encounters with the Roman legion, caused the Roman military leadership to decide to end this Jewish war decisively. Although historical sources are not in unanimous agreement, it is clear that the Roman military understood that the Temple in Jerusalem was a paramount symbol intimately involved in this Jewish rebellion against Roman rule; and so, during the battle for Jerusalem, the Temple was burned by Roman legionnaires on the ninth day of the Hebrew month of *Av*, in the year 70 C.E.

The catastrophic loss of the religious center of the Jewish religion was devastating. With the loss of the Temple, Jews could no longer bring animal sacrifices. The priests and levites were instantly bereft of their theological and actual livelihood. Common Jews no longer could make the traditional pilgrimages to Jerusalem on the holidays of Passover, Shavuot, and Sukkot. Many Jews felt spiritually cut off from their connection to God and were in despair. Judaism might have faded away as a religion and the Jewish people might have been permanently assimilated into other religions and cultures had it not been for the Rabbis.

The Rabbis, who up until this time had not been acknowledged by the majority of Jews as the spiritual, religious leaders of the people, rescued the Jewish people and the Jewish religion from this catastrophic despair by patiently teaching that it was still possible to worship God—even with the loss of the Temple and animal sacrifices. As one Rabbinic text succinctly encapsulates this experience:

Rabban Yochanon ben Zakkai was once walking with his disciple Rabbi Yehoshua near Jerusalem after the destruction of the Temple.

Rabbi Yehoshua looked at the Temple ruins and said: "Alas for us! The place which atoned for the sins of the people Israel through the ritual of animal sacrifice lies in ruins!" Then Rabban Yochanon ben Zakkai spoke to him these words of comfort: "Be not grieved, my son. There is another way of gaining atonement. And what is this other way? We must now gain atonement through deeds of loving kindness." For it is written, "Lovingkindness I desire, not sacrifice." (Hosea 6:6) [Avot D'Rabbi Natan 11a—quoted in *Siddur Sim Shalom* (Prayerbook of the Conservative Movement), p. 14]

The Rabbis argued that although the Temple was no longer in existence and the animal sacrifices had ceased, it was still possible to worship God through prayer and the observance of other religious rituals, such as engaging in acts of charity, observing the dietary laws of *Kashrut,* praying, and keeping the Sabbath. The Rabbis transformed Jewish society in the aftermath of the failed revolt and the destruction of the Temple by taking the Torah, the most sacred text in Judaism, and reinterpreting it so as to be in consonance with their new, post-Temple reality. While the Torah speaks of the significance of animal sacrifices, the Rabbis declared that prayer was an appropriate and acceptable substitute. They even found additional texts in other parts of the Bible, such as the prophets in the example given above, to demonstrate that God actually prefers acts of loving kindness and prayer to sacrifices. Such a massive shift and transformation of Jewish life did not occur immediately; but over several generations, the religious and legal culture of the Rabbis prevailed, and Rabbinic Judaism was largely accepted as the only form of legitimate Judaism.

The traditions and reinterpretations of the Torah, which the Rabbis expounded, were long maintained in an oral, verbal format so as to distinguish their teachings from the Torah—the written Torah. But over many generations, the traditions of the Rabbis also came to be written down and preserved in such great classical Rabbinic works as the *Mishnah,* the *Gemara,* various books of *Midrash,* and successive codes of Jewish law. While the Torah remained the supreme source of divinity and authenticity, the Rabbinic works reinterpreted the Torah so as to provide continuous religious and spiritual meaning to Jews in the new post-Temple world. And these Rabbinic works began to be studied with as much fervor and devotion as the Torah itself.

An imprecise, but apt analogy that helps to clarify the relationship between the Torah and the various works of Rabbinic literature is to compare the Torah to the U.S. Constitution. The Torah and the U.S. Constitution contain the core legal values of the Jewish tradition and the American government respectively. Although the Torah is understood to be divine, the U.S. Constitution is similarly venerated and treasured by the American people. However, the Constitution does not represent the totality of American law. From the beginning of U.S. history, Congress has written and adopted laws intended to further express the principles of the Constitution and to apply it to new situations that the Constitutional framers could not have foreseen. In addition, the Supreme Court has been charged with interpreting and often reinterpreting the Constitution when conflicts of interpretation have arisen. In this way, American law has continued to grow and evolve over the past two centuries in response to external reality but always based on the Constitution and its core values.

Similarly, Jewish law has continued to grow and evolve since the destruction of the Temple in the year 70 C.E. in response to the experiences of the Jewish people wherever they have lived throughout the past two thousand years. But this expanding corpus of Jewish law has always been based on the Torah and its core values. While it is possible to read the U.S. Constitution and understand a great deal about American law and government, this does not present the whole picture. Much has happened since the Constitution was enacted that has affected the development of American law and the U.S. government. This is true of Judaism as well. While it is possible to read the Torah and understand a great deal about Judaism, it is still not the whole picture. The Torah represents only the sacred core of Judaism, but Jewish laws and customs have continued to evolve and develop over time. In fact, Judaism has continued to grow and evolve so much that some today might not even recognize the similarities between the Torah and Rabbinic Judaism. Jewish communities and Rabbis all over the world throughout the past

two thousand years have continued to add to, expand, interpret, adapt, modify, and change the vast body of Jewish traditions, customs, laws, and rituals so that it will remain holy
and relevant to all Jews throughout time and all over the
world. The common denominator that unifies all of these different interpretations of the Jewish tradition is that they are
all derived from the Torah and the Rabbinic interpretations of
the Torah.

For the past two thousand years, with some minor excep-
tions, the overwhelming majority of Jews have been Rabbinic
Jews, not Biblical Jews. The customs and laws practiced by
Jews today are largely Rabbinic in origin. It is crucial that
Jewish students understand this reality because it is not
widely known or understood among Jews and non-Jews. One
of the ways to judge the success of Jewish education is to what
extent the graduates will be able to explain Judaism to fellow
Jews and to the outside world. And understanding the difference between the Biblical Israelite religion and modern
Rabbinic Judaism is an important touchstone for assessing
this success.

Knowledge vs. Skills

One of my students once proudly informed me that he had studied many Rabbinic texts in his previous *yeshiva* (Orthodox Jewish day school) and that he had a solid Jewish Studies background. And, indeed, when we studied various chapters of the *Mishnah* and the *Gemara* that he had learned previously, he knew the texts very well and was able to offer many insights. However, when we began to study new texts, which he had not previously studied, he was at a loss as to how to proceed. What he knew, he knew well. But what he didn't know, he didn't even know how to go about beginning to study. This student had an extensive body of Jewish knowledge and experience in studying Rabbinic texts, he knew a great deal about Jewish texts and had studied quite a lot of them, but he had never acquired text study skills. He had always been walked through the texts by his teachers, provided with translations and explanations and merely required to memorize this information. Is this what Jewish educators are looking for in their graduates from Jewish day schools and Jewish educational programs?

This is the wrong approach to Jewish education, especially for non-Orthodox Jewish students, who will probably be more intimately involved in the outside, secular world. The knowledge they learn must be sufficient to enable them to function as self-reliant, independent students of the Jewish tradition. Therefore, courses in Biblical and Rabbinic literature should emphasize text study skills more than the memorization of Jewish knowledge, no matter how crucial such information may be in practicing Judaism. Students should be encouraged to learn how to learn traditional texts on their own, to become independent learners. It should be the role of educators to help students acquire these skills for themselves, not by providing them with the translations and explanations, but rather, by showing them how to locate the information they need on their own. Then, once they have done all they can to translate and explain the texts on their own, teachers should review the texts in a group or a class so that they can construct the meaning and possible explanations of the text together. Of course, this could also lead to the opposite, equally unfortunate result that students might know how to study Biblical or Rabbinical texts, but never have learned enough background information to provide them with a foundation for this independent study. The ideal goal should be to find a compromise between students learning crucial, background information and acquiring sufficient text study skills for independent inquiry.

How can teachers go about doing this? The essential foundations of knowledge must be identified as well as the most important text study skills. Such knowledge and skills must be dependent on the age of the students and must take into account their previous Jewish education. As teachers create their own curricula, it is important for them to be aware of and familiar with some of the major areas of Jewish text study. The following is a selective survey of some of the major subject areas that can and should be included in Jewish Studies curricula. This survey is included here in order to provide enough information to help educators decide what kinds of texts they may want to include in their lesson plans. Here are some of the common, major areas of Jewish Studies in many formats of Jewish education:

Bible. The Bible is not a monolithic literary work. In fact, the Hebrew word for the Bible is *Tanakh* (תנ״ך), an acrostic of the Hebrew letters *Tav* (ת), *Nun* (נ), and *Chaf* (ך), which are the first letters of the three main sections of the Hebrew Bible: *Torah* (Instruction), *Neviim* (Prophets), and *Ketuvim* (Writings).

- *Torah.* Familiarity with the Bible might include knowledge of the Torah, specifically, the major narrative events and significant legal passages. In addition to studying the Torah from purely spiritual, moral, and religious perspectives, it is also possible to include the study of the literary value of the Torah, or its historical, or even cultural, value. Study of the Torah can also be used to approach important topics in modern religious studies, such as Science vs. Creationism, the study of ancient mythology, literary criticism, and the Documentary Hypothesis. The study of the Torah often includes the various interpretations of the Torah as recorded by the classical medieval commentators on the Torah, such as Rashi (Rabbi Shlomo Yitzchaki), Abraham Ibn Ezra, Ramban (Rabbi Moshe ben Nachman), and others.

- *Prophets and Writings.* Two major approaches that are often emphasized in the study of the prophets are the historical chronicles of the Former Prophets (Joshua, Judges, Samuel, and Kings) as well as the moral and religious development of the people of Israel as represented through the writings of the Later Prophets (Isaiah, Jeremiah, Ezekiel, and the twelve minor prophets). Units can be divided according the *Haftorah* selections for synagogue use, or book by book. Studies of the Writings frequently focus on the five Scrolls (Song of Songs, Ruth, Lamentations, Eccelesiastes, and Esther), which are read in synagogues as part of the yearly liturgical cycle, as well as the various spiritual and moral guidance contained in the Books of Psalms and Proverbs.

Rabbinics. This is a huge area of study encompassing the literary activity of the Rabbis specifically during late Antiquity (the later Roman and Byzantine empires), but it can include medieval and modern Rabbinic literature as well. The largest distinction that can be made in the knowledge of Rabbinic literature is between legal texts, which focus on the ritual, civil, and criminal laws of the Jewish people (*Halakha*), and the more imaginative, creative genres of literature, which include stories, fables, biographical incidents, legends, and folktales (*Aggada*).

- *Halakha.* The major Halakhic texts of Rabbinic literature are the *Mishnah,* the earliest formulation of Jewish law, and the *Gemara,* a commentary and expansion of the *Mishnah.* Together, these two works are known as the Talmud. Major medieval Rabbinic texts include the *Mishneh Torah* and the *Shulkhan Arukh,* which are later codifications of Jewish law. These works organize and explain the entire corpus of practical Jewish law that modern rabbis use as resources in shaping Jewish law today.

- *Aggada.* The major works of Aggada are commentaries and homiletical expansions of the Bible. Each major Biblical book has its own Aggadic volume, which contains an anthology of various Rabbinic interpretations and sermonic material. The works contain the theological ideas of the Rabbis of the Rabbinic period and represent a vast, rich archive of Jewish philosophy, stories, fables, parables, sayings, interpretations, explanations, biographical information about the Rabbis, and semihistorical descriptions of events from ancient times.

Jewish History. The study of Jewish History is often difficult to separate from the study of Biblical and Rabbinic texts as well as Jewish

Philosophy. However, it is possible to divide Jewish History into some broad periods: the Biblical period, the Rabbinic (or Talmudic) period, the Medieval period (when Jews lived under the political rule of Christianity and Islam), the modern period (beginning with the political emancipation of Jews in Europe), and the Contemporary period, including the origin of Zionism and the history of the State of Israel. Jewish History is rarely taught in many formats of Jewish education except for occasional units on the Holocaust, the birth of the modern state of Israel, or early Biblical periods. However, it is important that Jewish students learn as much Jewish History as possible because it is literally the story of where they come from. Public schools seldom include information about Jews or Judaism in their general history courses. Jewish students should know far more about their own history than simply where Jews "fit" in with the history of other peoples and civilizations. Jews have their own stories to communicate.

Hebrew Language. It is important that students develop the ability to hold an extended conversation on a variety of topics in the Hebrew language; read Biblical, Rabbinic, and modern Hebrew texts; and express themselves legibly in written Hebrew. The issue of Hebrew language as the language of instruction is dealt with extensively elsewhere; however, whether students are taught other subjects in Hebrew or not, Jewish students must be able minimally to read and write Hebrew and be familiar with a basic vocabulary.

Jewish Philosophy/Theology. Although closely related to Bible, Rabbinics, and Jewish History, it is possible to break down the development of Jewish philosophical and theological thought into several broad areas:

- *Biblical Theology.* This subject can cover the development of Israelite theology through an examination of the various books of the Bible. It includes how the Israelites developed an increasingly sophisticated understanding of God and their relationship to God throughout history. It also includes studying how the Israelites understood the concepts and reality of sin and punishment, exile and redemption on a personal and national level.

- *Rabbinic Theology.* This subject can cover the expansion of Jewish thought through the study of pertinent Talmudic and Midrashic texts that deal with the theological speculation of the Rabbis. The Rabbis had much to say about God, cosmology, theology, divine justice, death, resurrection, what constitutes the "good" life, charity, spirits, angels, and a wide variety of other relevant topics. Studying Rabbinic theology can provide a unique and consistent approach to studying a bewildering assortment of texts from Rabbinic works.

- *Medieval Philosophy.* This era can be broadly characterized as the development and confrontation between the Rationalist vs. Mystical understanding of God and the Jewish tradition, which occupied many rabbis and scholars for centuries. In other words, was God beyond human understanding, as the mystics asserted, or were God and God's ways capable of being comprehended, in however limited a way, by humans? This would also include the conflict between the Karaites and the Rabbinites, who held wildly divergent views as to what constitutes the essence of God's communication to the Jewish people. Was it the Torah alone, as the Karaites asserted, or did it also include the vast body of additional traditions and interpretations contained in the Oral Law (i.e., Rabbinic literature)?

- *Modern Philosophy.* This era can be broadly characterized as the development and the confrontation between the Hasidic movement and the *Mitnagdim* ("the opposers" of the Hasidim). The *Hasidim,* literally, the "pious," emphasized the cosmic relevance of performing everyday ritual activities and the role that joy, dancing, and alcohol can play in elevating the souls and spirits of Jews. The *Mitnagdim* objected to the entire basis and movement of the *Hasidim* and, instead, emphasized an intellectual, scholarly approach to Jewish life. The study of modern Jewish philosophy also includes the development of the *Musar* ("ethical") Movement, that is, a trend in Eastern European Torah academies that emphasized moral and ethical behavior, as well as the origin of Zionism. The history of Zionism includes both intellectual thinkers who began to popularize the concept of a Jewish homeland to save Jews from antisemitism in Europe, as well as the political figures who presaged and postdated Theodor Herzl, the founder of political Zionism.

- *Contemporary Philosophy.* This subject could focus on the origins of denominationalism in Europe and the United States. Contemporary Jewish philosophy deals with the *Haskala,* or the Jewish "enlightenment" and the political emancipation of Jews in Europe. These events led to the development of the Reform, Orthodox, and Neo-Orthodox movements in Europe, which later became established in the United States where continued developments led to the creation of the Conservative and Reconstructionist movements.

In addition to clarifying a selection of major topics of Jewish Studies classes, it is also important to identify the major study skills that students can be taught in order to facilitate their growth as independent learners of the Jewish tradition. So as to take advantage of the wealth of Hebrew texts in the Bible and Rabbinic literature, students should develop the following text study skills.

- *Hebrew Language.* As described previously, for students to become independent learners of the Jewish tradition, they must develop their abilities to read, comprehend, and write in Hebrew. Because the majority of the classical Jewish sources are in Hebrew, students must have the capacity to interact with original sources and not merely to study them in translation. Even if they never develop fluency in Hebrew, it is vital that students feel that they possess the skills to interact directly with the original texts of the Jewish tradition in order to build up their sense of Jewish authenticity and adequacy in relating to the classical Hebrew texts in Judaism.

- *Dictionary Skills/Habits (Translation).* As it is often not possible for non-native Hebrew speakers to become completely conversant in all of the various forms of Hebrew and Hebrew grammar that are used in the Bible and Rabbinic literature, it is important that students develop the habits and skills necessary to consult all of the relevant reference works to aid their studies. This includes familiarity with Hebrew–English dictionaries, technical references such as Biblical concordances and indices, encyclopedias, and various textual guides that can help students learn the meaning of technical words and phrases and common Biblical and Rabbinic legal and cultural concepts. Students should also be current with CD-ROM sources and internet technology and programs so as to be able to utilize all of the resources available.

- *Navigation Skills/Knowledge of the Major Texts.* It is important that students develop the skills necessary to navigate and locate various subjects in the Bible, *Mishnah, Talmud,* Midrashic works, Rambam's *Mishneh Torah, Shulkhan Arukh,* and other sources. In order for students to be truly independent learners of the Jewish tradition, they must know first where to locate the relevant texts of study. Whereas a student may have studied *Mishnah* previously, he or she might not know where to find Mishnaic material about other topics. The *Gemara* is arranged according to a very unique system of pagination; the *Mishneh Torah* is divided up differently from the Talmud, as is the *Shulkhan Arukh.* Therefore, it is of incalculable value for Jewish educators to present overviews and structural diagrams and information to students about what kinds of topics are found in which texts and how to go about finding them, whether in Hebrew or in English translation. Often, the mere presentation of such material can be an effective means for teaching students about the broad range of subjects included in the Jewish tradition. Frequently, students are unaware of what the major works of the Jewish tradition are and what subjects are dealt with in them. Acquiring a survey-level understanding of the classical sources should be required in Jewish Studies courses.

- *Literary Genre.* Just as important as knowing where to find different subjects within different texts is the ability actually to study the texts once they have been located. Studying Torah is a very different enterprise than studying Talmud because they are two very different kinds of literature. It is important that students be knowledgeable about the different genres of Jewish literature that they may encounter in their studies. For example, in studying the Torah, students should learn a little about the different literary genres common in the Bible, such as theme words and conventions of Biblical narrative; they should be able to recognize and understand the casuistic (case law) and apodictic (universal) formats of legal codes and the structure of parallelism that defines Biblical poetry. Just as students learn to read and understand fiction and nonfiction, novels, plays, newspapers, and science fiction, Jewish students must learn the similar major literary distinctions within the Jewish tradition.

- *Outlining (Structure).* Jewish texts are not always organized in a manner that is readily understandable. Especially in Rabbinic literature, Rabbis quote other Rabbis from earlier generations; the language of the text switches back and forth between Hebrew and Aramaic; and short, technical and obscure phrases can contain information crucial for understanding the logic of a passage. A key component in learning to comprehend such texts is the ability to outline and create a logical structure from the text. Sometimes, simply diagramming the sequence of ideas in a text can yield previously obscure insights. For example, in Rabbinic literature, students can be taught how to identify simple statements, questions, objections, and resolutions. Identifying and labeling such elements can be very helpful for students in understanding the flow of Rabbinic texts. This is an important skill for Jewish students to master because it helps them to understand the texts in depth.

- *Textual Analysis (Critical Analysis).* After a text has been located, translated, and outlined, its meaning can still remain elusive. Students of Jewish texts must also develop skills of critical analysis. This means asking such questions as, Who wrote this text? Why? What was their purpose in recording this event or idea? Who were they writing it for? What did they hope would happen as a result of others reading this text? Students should then try to generate answers based on either their own research in encyclopedias and history texts or with information provided by the teachers. Learning to take a step or two back from a text is also a crucial critical analysis skill that enables students to more fully comprehend a text. These are sophisticated skills that Jewish students must also cultivate to enable them to be independent learners.

Mastering a particular body of Jewish knowledge is a valuable step in becoming a lifelong learner of the Jewish tradition. However, if students are not taught to develop the skills with which to continue their studies, such knowledge remains isolated and largely inapplicable to different areas of Jewish life. As teachers develop their own curricula appropriate for their classrooms, settings, and students, they should keep in mind the various options for topics in Jewish Studies as well as the kinds of text analysis skills. Does the acquisition of Jewish knowledge take precedence over the development of text study skills? In my opinion, it is more important that students be taught Jewish Studies in a way that will help them acquire text study skills. Developing solid Jewish study skills can help students attain competence and confidence in being able to locate and learn about nearly any topic or Jewish text they may be interested in exploring.

TEXT-DRIVEN VS. CONTENT-DRIVEN CURRICULA

What will best cover the desired information in any given Jewish Studies class—a text-based curriculum that is organized so as to follow the meandering terrain of the Rabbinic or Biblical texts under discussion? Or perhaps a curriculum consisting of shorter, more topical textual selections drawn freely from a wide variety of different works and genres based on the topic(s) of the course is a better organizational format? Many Jewish educators assert the value of picking one or two central Biblical or Rabbinic texts, studying them in depth, and basing the subject of the course and text skills on those that one encounters in the journey. However, other educators maintain that the advantages of custom-designed, focused curricula far outweigh the more traditional text-based format of study. There are advantages and disadvantages to each form.

Text-driven curricula have a number of advantages in Jewish Studies classes:

- Text-driven curricula can, in some ways, be considered more "natural" in that they follow the flow of the text itself. Students must be prepared to deal with and learn all of the various subjects and varied genres of literature, Biblical or Rabbinic, which they may encounter in the focused and extended study of a single text. It is also the more typical way that texts have been studied in the past.

- Text-driven curricula are easier for teachers to prepare and teach because they follow the progression of the text itself. While other texts and materials can be used to supplement the extended study of a single text, it is relatively effortless to follow one text and its attendant commentaries. It is also much easier for students to bring to class only one book or sourcebook that contains the one text they are studying.

- The study of text-driven curricula enable students to discover insights into the composition and depth of a single text. Studying one text as an integrated, whole, complete unit of study gives students the ability to gain familiarity with Biblical or Rabbinic texts overall. Learning the ebb and flow of a text, its main ideas and digressions, helps students learn the general literary geography of a particular work and develop an appreciation for the text as a

- Text-driven curricula require the development of a wide variety of textual skills and the building of a vast technical vocabulary. Studying a single text provides a wealth of different textual challenges for students to master; therefore, they must become adept at dealing with whatever the text may "throw" at them. As every Biblical and Rabbinic text makes use of its own highly specialized vocabulary and constellation of self-referential terms, studying a single text provides students with an opportunity to attain fluency in the particular morphology of any given work.

Despite these advantages to teaching text-driven curricula, there are also a number of disadvantages to this approach that limit its effectiveness and success.

- Text-driven curricula can be chaotic in that there may be no coherence of themes in the text chosen. For example, the Biblical book of Exodus may be relatively simple to follow; however, one encounters in it a variety of disparate literary genres, such as narratives, poetry, legal codes, and technical descriptions of the Tabernacle. Similarly, while one can pick a single Tractate of Talmud to study, even a relatively focused work, such as the *Mishnah*, is not without its share of tangents and digressions. Teachers must then decide how much time they want to devote to pursuing and explaining these tangents and digressions, or how much time they want to take to clarify the extraneous concepts and topics. If they choose to provide the students with as complete an understanding of a text as possible, that may require spending significant time clarifying subtle or abstruse points while neglecting the main text and topic. On the other hand, if a teacher chooses continually to advance in the main text without taking the time to elucidate puzzling hints and references, students may end up with a confused, incomplete, or superficial understanding of a text.
- Text-driven curricula do not allow students to develop a coherent or focused set of text study skills. For example, it is helpful for students to compare and contrast a selection of poetic sections from the Torah in order to learn about the overall structure and genre of Biblical poetry. However, students may only encounter one or two such sections in the study of any single Biblical book. Similarly, it is important for students to study a selection of distinct and characteristic Rabbinic questions in order to grasp typical Talmudic methodology. However, there is no guarantee that any given chapter of *Mishnah* or *Gemara* will contain enough

examples of a particular kind of Rabbinic argument for students to learn in depth and have the opportunity to master the approach or feel comfortable or capable of studying such texts again in the future.

- Text-driven curricula are too wide and varied to offer any assurance that the subjects covered or the text skills required will be relevant (or of interest) to students. The relevance of the subject and its interest to students depend upon the book or chapter of any given text. One of the typical features of the Talmud, for example, is that it seems to be characterized by digressions and tangents as opposed to staying focused on any particular topic. As a result, students may never develop the skills to identify, analyze, and understand typical Rabbinic argument structures because a given text may contain only one or two examples despite the fact that the Talmud, as a whole, may be filled with such argument structures. For instance, the Rabbinic hermeneutical tool known as "Kal V'Homer," or an "a fortiori" inference, in which two cases are compared to one another, one lenient and one strict, is a fairly commonplace argument. However, there is no guarantee that a given chapter will contain enough examples of these arguments for students to easily recognize and understand them. Similarly, while a Talmudic chapter may putatively begin on one topic, it may wander and digress so widely so that students no longer remember (or care) what they are learning about anymore.

- Text-driven curricula are more difficult to prepare because the teacher must master all of the various subjects and concepts that any given text may contain, including all digressions. Just as it is difficult for students to follow and master a chapter of Talmud or an entire book of the Torah, teachers must become experts in all of the subjects mentioned in passing and be prepared to provide additional materials that will help clarify such details and digressions to their students.

- Text-driven curricula can't be tailored to class needs or interests because they follow the flow of a text. Although a teacher can choose a particular Biblical book or tractate of Talmud based on its overall theme, as was mentioned previously, there is often tangential material that may diverge significantly from the apparent topic of the book or chapter. One of the chief complaints of many students in all formats of Jewish education is that their Jewish Studies don't seem to be pertinent or are boring. Picking and sticking with only one text limits the ability of a teacher to create a course that is of greater relevance to the students and their interests.

- Text-driven curricula may make it difficult for students to perceive larger thematic structures and themes in a text. When students study any given text in great detail, they tend to lose the forest for the trees. Caught up in the struggle to make sense of difficult texts on a line-by-line basis for extended periods of time, they tend to magnify the micro to the detriment of the macro of a text. And because of the tangential nature of so many Jewish texts, students can often lose sight of the original topic of the text.

In contrast, content-driven curricula address and resolve many of the problems detailed previously. In fact, they are probably better suited to the educational environment of non-Orthodox Jewish day schools, synagogue religious schools, and supplementary schools. Nevertheless, such courses have their own share of disadvantages.

- Content-driven curricula are difficult for teachers to prepare as they must track down a wide variety of relevant sources in order to create a coherent curriculum. For instance, to create a unit or a course on *Tzedaka,* charity, a teacher must have the appropriate encyclopedias, indices, reference works, or CD-ROM computer disks that will help them locate all of the relevant citations. The teacher must have access to all of these primary sources and have the time and ability to find all of these selections in each of the works cited. For instance, there are sources about Jewish laws regarding charity in the Torah, *Mishnah, Gemara,* and numerous works of Rabbinic *Midrash.* Therefore, such courses demand a great deal of expertise with many texts as well as time to find, copy, and organize the sources in a coherent format. Creating sourcebooks is a significant undertaking and requires much dedication and commitment on the part of a teacher who wants to create his or her own new Jewish Studies course.

- Content-driven curricula may also be difficult to teach. Even if a teacher doesn't create his or her own content-driven curriculum, it may be difficult for the teacher to teach such a course as he or she must keep the text study and class discussions focused on the chosen topic. In other words, content-driven classes may potentially suffer from the exact opposite problem of text-driven courses, namely, too exclusive a focus on the chosen topic, which may also cause a loss of interest among students. Such courses must balance a focus on the topic with a sufficient variety of subtopics so as to keep students interested and on task.

- Content-driven curricula can also be "choppy" in that there is often no continuity in the genre of texts chosen for study. A curriculum may include texts from the Torah, *Mishnah, Gemara,* Midrashic works, as well as Halakhic codifications and Responsa literature, all jumbled together. Although they may be well organized according to theme and topic, the mixture of different literary types of Rabbinic texts can make for a confusing presentation of selections. The Hebrew vocabulary can vary significantly from text to text as can the technical terms and concepts used in each one. Also, it is sometimes difficult to understand Rabbinic texts in isolation from their context, having been taken out of the natural flow of their subject.

However, in spite of these minor disadvantages, content-driven curricula are far better vehicles for teaching Jewish Studies than are text-driven curricula. This is so because:

- Content-driven curricula can be tailored so as to present the exact texts and ideas that a teacher may wish to present. Freed from having to include extraneous material that may be off topic but nonetheless is embedded in a text, the teacher can select texts to help illuminate specific aspects and themes of Biblical or Rabbinic literature. It is possible to connect ideas and themes that may be scattered throughout the Bible, Talmud, or works of *Midrash* when they are all presented together.

- Content-driven curricula are often easier to understand because the texts have been customized in order to present a smooth, logical progression of ideas. The greatest advantage is that a teacher can present the selections in a form that will best enable the students to understand the development of an idea or theme, whether it be in chronological order or thematic order. Parallel texts can be placed side by side so as to make clear similarities and contrasts or arranged on a page in such a way as to reveal certain ideas and interpretations.

- Content-driven curricula can also bring out larger themes in Biblical and Rabbinic literature. By including selections from a variety of different Talmudic tractates, books of *Midrash,* or Biblical books, it is possible to draw students' attention to broad themes and concepts in the Jewish tradition. For example, it is not always possible to understand the concept of Divine Justice when students study individual Biblical books and Talmudic and

Midrashic chapters. However, teachers can create customized units that will pull together related texts from many different works; this will, in fact, make it clear that there has been an extensive and subtle development of this theological tenet beginning in Biblical times and extending through Rabbinic times.

- Content-driven curricula can make Jewish Studies classes more relevant and interesting to students by focusing on specific topics that may be of current interest. Rabbinic literature is notoriously diffuse, with many related texts and ideas often scattered throughout different tractates of the Talmud and books of *Midrash.* A course based on content and themes has the advantage of presenting only those relevant, related texts.

- Content-driven curricula are also often easier for a teacher to teach because the texts are all related and focused on a particular subject or theme. While it may be difficult to create such courses and sourcebooks, they are easier to present to students because there are no built-in digressions or tangents that would have to be taught simply because they happen to be found in a text. It is possible to teach a more focused, coherent class on any given theme or subject.

Both text-driven and content-driven course formats are effective means of organizing Jewish Studies courses, depending upon the goals of a teacher and the course. Content-driven curricula are good for students who have few text study skills in order to be able to see the coherence of broad themes; conversely, they work well for students who are well equipped to study a variety of texts and are better able to understand the different genres of the texts presented. Text-driven curricula are also good for students who either have limited text study skills and need to develop better ones or, ironically enough, for students who are competent in text study and want to gain a greater mastery of a particular text, chapter, book, or tractate. However, it is important to bear in mind that each format has its unique advantages and disadvantages but that content-driven curricula are more flexible and adaptable to a greater variety of settings for Jewish education.

DEPTH VS. BREADTH

Is it better to devote an entire year of Bible studies to a close and intensive reading of the first three chapters of the book of Genesis, or is it a better to study all of Genesis, Exodus, and the Five Megillot in that year and cover more material? Which is better: in-depth study of a little or superficial study of a lot? Depth or breadth? This is an important issue to deal with in Jewish Studies because it impacts all aspects of the teaching of Jewish Studies classes from classroom management issues to curriculum development. There are advantages and disadvantages to each approach; however, given the nature of the American liberal Jewish community (i.e., the non-Orthodox world) it is important that students learn as much as possible within the time constraints of all Jewish educational formats—even if it is somewhat more superficial—rather than have in-depth, but limited knowledge about the Jewish tradition.

Why would anyone ever choose to devote months and months to the study of just a few chapters of Torah? Many teachers prefer to spend a great deal of time on a limited number of texts for a number of reasons. The first is that by doing so it is possible to fully explore and develop educationally all aspects of the texts. Spending a year on the first three chapters of Genesis enables students to master the Hebrew texts and gain a great deal of familiarity with all the details of the stories. Students can learn the literary structure of the chapters dealing with the creation of the world, determine how they interrelate with one another, and discuss the implications of these comparisons and contrasts. Students can also study the actual historical evidence of these events, the creation myths of different cultures, and how modern Jews can and should relate to these stories. There is time to explore the traditional Rabbinic commentaries on the texts and examine the insights they provide. Students can be encouraged to explore the theological implications to the texts and further develop their own philosophical reactions.

Second, spending so much time on a few texts enables students to feel that they have fully mastered a certain part

of the Jewish tradition. Part of the purpose of Jewish education is to build up a student's sense of religious competency.
Knowing a Hebrew text, its literary details, Rabbinic commentaries, historical evidence, and its theological implications provides students with a greater sense of confidence and
adequacy as Jews. Students do, indeed, know a great deal
about the texts they have studied when they spend so much
time on them; and this can build up their self-esteem in terms
of their Jewish identity.

Finally, many teachers spend a great deal of time on few
texts because it is easier. Preparing for a larger number of texts
takes a lot of time and energy as teachers must master more
material themselves before presenting it to students. Limiting
the texts means reducing the time and energy spent on preparation. It also creates a "comfort zone" for teachers when they
can spend months on the same, familiar stories and simply
generate new angles of approach and analysis for their students to explore. Limiting the texts also ensures that a teacher
will never have too little time to cover the curriculum. After
all, less ambitious goals are more easily achieved.

However, devoting so much time to few texts and topics is
problematic because it ultimately undermines the very goals
that teachers are trying to achieve by adopting this approach.
Spending a great deal of time on few texts actually increases
a student's sense of ignorance of the Jewish tradition because
it unintentionally emphasizes the vast majority of the texts
and topics that students do not cover in their Jewish Studies
classes. Learning only the first three chapters of Genesis in an
entire year in a course devoted to covering the entire book
ensures that students will not have the time, or perhaps the
opportunity in the future, to study the remaining forty-seven
chapters. This approach ensures that students do, indeed,
know a lot—but, unfortunately, about a very little.

Covering topics in depth, as opposed to in breadth, can
also potentially create a sense of trepidation in students
about encountering new, unfamiliar material. Having grown
accustomed to spending a great deal of time on a few texts,
students may feel a sense of inadequacy when confronted
with new texts that are not presented in as much depth or
detail as they have previously learned them. If students feel

that they have not learned a text in as much depth as they have become accustomed to, they may feel all the more uncomfortable with new texts that they learn but in less depth. In other words, if their internal standards of what constitutes "real" text study are based on a time-intensive approach, future text study may not stand up to this rigorous standard. As such, they may never feel that they are capable of mastering the texts they study in the future. This may only increase their sense of inadequacy when it comes to their overall Jewish education.

This is true because, for the most part, a great many liberal (i.e., non-Orthodox) Jews that I have come into contact with or taught, including children, teenagers, and even adults, are struggling to combat a sense of Jewish illegitimacy when it comes to assessing their sense of Jewish adequacy. No matter how fluent in Hebrew students may be, how proficient they may be in leading prayer and living Jewish lives, or how extensive their knowledge of both Biblical and Rabbinic texts, a disturbingly too many of them compare themselves to their Orthodox counterparts and feel that they are inadequate. They somehow feel inauthentic and ignorant in comparison. As a result, it is imperative that all formats of Jewish education aid all students in feeling that they can compete in the world of Jewish knowledge. While focusing on a small number of texts may provide a wealth of Jewish knowledge, which many students may even acknowledge is not covered in Orthodox institutions of Jewish study, I have found that the depth of these courses still cannot successfully compete in students' minds with courses that cover material in greater breadth. In-depth study further marginalizes and limits what the students do know about the Jewish tradition by confining their studies to limited, selected portions of Jewish texts. Psychologically, however, students seem to feel a greater sense of mastery and Jewish competency when they are familiar with a greater number of texts.

In-depth study classes can also lead to classroom management problems because students may not feel they are covering sufficient ground and may become bored in class. While no curriculum should ever be entirely student-interest driven, successful educators must adapt to the classroom situation and take student reactions into account when creating curriculum. Spending too much time on limited texts or topics can sap student motivation and lose their interest. A fellow teacher was experiencing some classroom problems because his students were growing restless due to the pace of his class. Despite the fact that the course syllabus described the class as covering all of Genesis and Exodus, his students were unhappy with the fact that they were only studying the story of the Binding of Isaac (Genesis, chapter 22) and it was coming up on Purim (around mid-March)! Recognizing that his pace was causing a lack of interest and listlessness in class, he condensed the next several topics into short, mini-units and brought his students up to the book of Exodus for the latter part of the second semester of the course. Although his students were somewhat overwhelmed by the unfamiliar, fast pace, they enjoyed the new material and felt as though they were finally learning new material at a rate that was more challenging and engaging.

Covering more Jewish Studies texts and topics as opposed to in-depth study addresses many of the concerns raised previously. However, covering Genesis, Exodus, and the Five Megillot (Song of Songs, Ruth, Lamentations, Ecclesiastes, and Esther) in a single academic year is also not without its problems. Covering so much material in so (relatively) short a time means that the texts and topics will be presented somewhat superficially. However, what this really means is that teachers must make decisions about the priority of which texts they want to read and what topics they want to include. As it is not really possible to teach all of Genesis, Exodus, and the Five Megillot in any degree of seriousness or depth in a single academic year, when I taught this course, I had to make difficult decisions about what to include and what to exclude.

As it was clear that I would not be able to teach every chapter of both Genesis and Exodus in a single year, I decided to choose several major narratives from each book to focus on those that were particularly important and characteristic of each book. For example, I chose seven subjects from Genesis: the story of creation, the story of the Garden of Eden, Noah and the flood, God's call to Abraham, the binding of

Isaac, the deception stories of Jacob, and the motifs of Joseph's story. These stories included characters and events with which I felt, subjectively, every Jewish student in a day school should be intimately familiar. I then selected approximately ten to twenty verses to study in depth with the students so that they would know key Hebrew verses, phrases, and vocabulary. While I focused on the simple, contextual meanings of the verses and stories (which is known as *peshat,* i.e., "simple"), I also chose a number of choice comments from Rashi, the classic Medieval Jewish commentator on the Torah so that the students would get a sense of how the Jewish tradition interpreted and explained these verses (i.e., the *drash,* or Rabbinic interpretations).

In addition, I felt that it was vital that educated Jews should be familiar with, or at least exposed to, some of the results of modern academic Biblical studies. Therefore, I paired each of the seven stories and topics from the book of Genesis (and Exodus as well) with matching scholarly topics. For instance, after having studied the creation stories in Genesis, students also spent time learning about and discussing the theories of evolution versus the modern fundamentalist interpretation of Genesis known as "creationism." Paired with the Garden of Eden story was a unit on what constitutes myth and what we can learn from mythology: namely, that while a Biblical story may not necessarily be historically accurate as a factual description of events, it can still be "true" in that it comments upon and provides etiologies for universal truths about human life. Paired with the stories of Noah and the flood, students were introduced to the Documentary Hypothesis and compared and contrasted apparently parallel versions of the flood stories. Paired with the stories of Abraham and the binding of Isaac (as well as the Joseph stories), students learned how to analyze Biblical narratives based on word motifs and recurring themes. Paired with the Jacob stories, students continued to apply the principles of literary analysis and also learned about the Rabbinic concept of "*Midah K'neged Midah,*" or "measure for measure": that is, the way one sins determines the manner in which he or she will be punished, or, as my students put it, "what goes around comes around!"

Therefore, while I was unable to cover all of the chapters in the books of Genesis, Exodus, or the Five Megillot, I was able to provide a strong foundation for Biblical studies for my students. They learned the basic details of major Biblical stories, some Hebrew verses, and Rabbinic commentaries, as well as modern critical academic approaches to Biblical studies. Indeed, there are a number of advantages to teaching Jewish Studies courses that sacrifice some in-depth study for breadth and scope of texts and topics. The first is that even if students do not cover a particular topic or text in depth, they have a basis for future reference and study in the future. If one of the goals of Jewish education is to provide them with a broad base of knowledge to build up their sense of Jewish competency and adequacy, students will have at least rudimentary knowledge of where to go and how to go about returning to study the texts and topics again. For example, the students in my Bible class on Genesis and Exodus acquired a significant overview of these books with sufficient information about major stories and characters such that, if they should be interested in studying these books again in the future, they have a substantial base of knowledge with which to begin. However, even if they choose not to study these texts again in the future, they were provided with a presentation of these topics sufficiently broad as well as in-depth to give them as adequate a knowledge of these Biblical books and subjects as they may need in the future.

The second advantage of broad study courses is that the students gain a sense of self-confidence and mastery of the material. Despite the fact that students in my Genesis and Exodus Bible class did not study every chapter or story in these books, they derived the satisfaction of learning these books in their entirety. While minor details may elude them, I was confident—as were my students—that they had learned a tremendous amount of material. Regarding Biblical studies in particular, it is especially important that Jewish students learn as much of the Bible as they can, because, as American Jews, we live in a Christian society where it is more than likely that our Christian neighbors are more familiar with the Hebrew Bible than we are. As a result, the less informed that Jews are about the Bible, especially the prophetic books, the more vulnerable they are to Christian missionizing at the worst, or simply to being misled about the contents of the Bible at the least.

Broad Jewish Studies courses also help reduce discipline and motivation issues among the students. As was mentioned previously, when students feel that they are not making any progress or not learning enough to challenge them, they often begin to express their frustration by acting out in class. Many classroom behavior issues can be traced to students not being sufficiently challenged. When students continuously whisper to one another, pass notes, or work on other class assignments during Jewish Studies classes, these may be indications that they are no longer interested in the material they are studying.

A fellow teacher once asked me to sit in on her class because she was experiencing chronic minor student disturbances. I saw students paying more attention to each other than to the teacher, doodling in the margins of their notebooks, and constantly asking irrelevant questions of the teacher about information that had just been presented but that they hadn't grasped because they hadn't been listening. I also noticed that the class had been dealing with the same material for some weeks and appeared bored with the topic. I recommended that the teacher pick up the pace, both in terms of presenting more new material at a quicker rate as well as her actual classroom teaching style. Rather than stopping to answer numerous questions about what had just been covered, I urged her to pepper her lectures and presentations with the phrase "You are responsible for this material whether you are listening or not." Within a week of adopting my recommendations, this teacher approached me to thank me for my advice. She was excited to report that the number of extraneous student questions had declined and that she was much further along in her curriculum than she had anticipated. While offering a greater breadth of materials as opposed to in-depth studies is no guarantee that students will stay focused on their studies or motivated to learn the material, it does require a more brisk classroom pace. A quicker pace minimally insures that students must pay somewhat more attention to what is transpiring in the classroom and that they must keep up with major assignments or risk falling behind or failing the course.

Finally, teaching Jewish Studies courses that cover more material indicates that a school, or individual teachers, acknowledge their own responsibility to provide students with as complete a Jewish education as possible, as opposed to giving up and citing time constraints for failure. Many teachers justify covering so little material by complaining about the lack of time devoted to Jewish Studies. Indeed, even in full-day Jewish schools, and especially in synagogue and supplementary schools, there is truly not enough time to impart to students of any age all of the information and texts they should be learning in order to lead competent Jewish lives and feel a sense of adequacy in their Jewish knowledge and practices. Given these legitimate time constraints, many teachers settle for less or rely on the hope that their students will yet learn with other teachers, who will make up what they have been missing in their class. In other words, they are relying on educational procrastination, hoping that there will still be time and other teachers who will get around to teaching Jewish students what they need to know.

Realistically, Jewish educators in all formats must acknowledge that there will never be enough time for Jewish Studies and that if they do not themselves accept the responsibility of giving their students the most complete and broad Jewish education they possibly can, no one else will. Every Jewish Studies teacher who teaches a class must adopt the attitude that he or she is the one who is going to teach the students everything they will need to know about the particular subject or text appropriate for the age of the students.

So is it better to devote an entire year of Bible studies to a close and intensive reading of the first three chapters of the book of Genesis, or is it a better to study all of Genesis, Exodus, and the Five Megillot in that year and cover more material? I believe that despite the advantages and disadvantages of each approach, it is more important that students be taught as much as possible given the time constraints of Jewish education. It is better that students know a little about a lot, rather than a lot about a little.

Hebrew as the Language of Instruction

Should Jewish Studies classes be taught in English or Hebrew? Or should only the actual texts be studied in Hebrew and subsequent discussion and analysis be conducted in English? Perhaps the texts should also be provided in English translation? These questions all revolve around the central issue of the role of Hebrew in Jewish Studies classes: namely, should Jewish educators sacrifice potential clarity in the classroom in their commitment to Hebrew language instruction to native English-speaking students, or should Hebrew be solely relegated to the Hebrew language classes? Of course these questions are dependent upon the level of Hebrew skills of the students involved. Yet, these questions regarding the role of Hebrew in Jewish education are the subject of intense debate in the world of Jewish education at this time.

Despite the different emphasis that each of the movements in American Jewish denominations and their schools place on the role and importance of Hebrew, the issue of Hebrew must be dealt with for a variety of reasons. The role of Hebrew will always be crucial to Jewish education because it is the language of the Bible and the majority of Rabbinic texts. Hebrew was the original language of discourse of the Israelites and their descendants, the Jews. The Rabbis who created the *Mishnah* spoke Hebrew and the Rabbis who created the *Gemara* also spoke Hebrew (although their primary language was Aramaic, a cognate of Hebrew). People who want to understand the context of the classic Jewish texts must study them in their original language.

Anyone who has ever studied another language knows that there are certain ideas and concepts that can only be understood in their original language. Some values are embedded in the very language of keywords and phrases in the Jewish tradition and cannot always be adequately translated or explained. For example, the Hebrew word *tzedakah* is often translated as charity. However, *tzedakah* does not actually mean "charity"; it means "justice." Charity comes from the Latin word *charitas,* which means "heart." Therefore, the concept of charity in English is considered voluntary because it comes from the heart. In Christianity, charity is something that people give when their heart moves them. In contrast, tzedakah/justice is a Rabbinic concept that embodies the idea that Jews are obligated to pursue social and economic justice. Jews must help the oppressed members of society as well as those in financial straits not because they may want to, but because they are required to. In addition, tzedakah is not limited to giving money; it involves actions and commitment beyond mere financial gifts. It is an obligation for Jews to engage in acts of tzedakah, not simply a "nice" thing to do because it stems from someone's heart. This is one example of how certain Biblical and Rabbinic concepts can only truly be understood in depth by comprehending their Hebrew meanings.

Hebrew is also the common language of the Jewish people today, throughout the world, as well as in the past throughout Jewish history. Wherever Jews live, the common language that any given Jew is bound to speak and that can unite them is Hebrew. Despite the general ignorance of Hebrew in the United States, it remains true that Jews from Argentina can only speak with Jews from Iran in Hebrew. Hebrew has been the lingua franca of Jews for literally thousands of years. No matter where Jews lived in historical times, the one language that, for instance, Jews of Portugal were able to use to communicate with Jews from Poland was Hebrew. Part of the reason that Hebrew has been the common language of Jews is that it is the language of Jewish prayer. No matter what the first language of Jews may be, the prayers they recite are in Hebrew. It is the language that encapsulates the hopes, dreams, and confessions of the Jewish people. When Jews travel around the world, they can always rely on the fact that the prayers they recite in any foreign synagogue will be in Hebrew. It is a powerful link that connects modern Jews with Jews who lived in Biblical times, through Rabbinic times, and up until the present day.

In modern times, Hebrew is also the language of the modern state of Israel. It is of practical use to know a spoken language of another country. However, Israel is not simply another foreign country, nor is Hebrew simply a foreign language to Jews. There are spiritual and theological reasons for Diaspora Jews to be familiar with and speak the language of the Jewish state. Whereas Yiddish or Ladino were once (and still are, in some cases) the first or second languages of the majority of Jews worldwide, Hebrew has become the most practical first or second language for Jews. It is also a matter of national and religious pride to have revived the esoteric language of the Bible and transformed it into a language of a modern nation.

The ability to read, write, and understand Hebrew has also become a touchstone of authenticity in terms of Jewish identity today. The more alienated and unfamiliar with Hebrew Jews are, the less connected and knowledgeable about Judaism they tend to be. Hebrew literacy is an expression of Jewish legitimacy and identity because many people understand Hebrew to be a vital component in transmitting Jewish values, culture, and identity to future generations. Because Hebrew is the original language of Jewish religious texts, the traditional language of the Jewish people, the language of the prayer book, and the language of the modern state of Israel, Hebrew plays a unique role in creating Jewish knowledge and identity. Therefore, for all of these reasons, Hebrew will always play a pivotal role in Jewish education.

The current debate about the role of Hebrew concerns whether non-language Jewish Studies classes—that is, those classes whose sole purpose is not to provide language instruction but to focus on Jewish content—should also be taught in Hebrew. Should Hebrew be the medium of instruction in these classes, or should it be confined to text study alone? That is, should the texts be taught in Hebrew but discussed in English, or should Jewish texts be taught in English translation? Aside from the emotional and political issues that are legitimately connected to this issue, it is important to highlight the educational effects of teaching Jewish Studies classes in Hebrew.

There are clearly a number of disadvantages to teaching Jewish Studies classes in Hebrew. First, most American Jews are not familiar with or fluent in Hebrew. Depending upon previous education, it has presumably been the goal of Jewish educators to assure that most Jews in a Jewish educational day-school system, religious school, or supplemental Hebrew school can at least read and write Hebrew and translate basic vocabulary words. However, when it comes to the comprehension, discussion, and analysis of Hebrew texts, many Jewish students simply cannot function in an all-Hebrew classroom environment. Despite the fact that many educators feel that language immersion is the best form of language acquisition, when it comes to learning a text-based, content course entirely in Hebrew, for nonspeakers, the language can be a barrier rather than an aid in promoting learning.

In order for students to succeed in this kind of environment, teachers must limit the depth and sophistication of text study and discussion, use simple vocabulary, restate key ideas with different Hebrew words in hope that students will understand, and, finally, repeat key concepts in English. All of these teaching methods take a great deal of time, which slows the pace of a class. The need to repeat information can become tedious for students and teachers alike, and the need to translate some words and phrases into English mitigates the effect of the all-Hebrew learning environment. It can also become boring for those students who are more familiar with Hebrew. The alternative to teaching at a slower pace, at a lower level, using frequent repetition and translation is that students become lost and unable to follow at the higher level of instruction. That being the case, they gain neither Hebrew proficiency nor the textual knowledge that is the purpose of Jewish Studies classes.

However, there are many advantages to using only Hebrew in Jewish Studies classes. The first is that it forces everyone to acquire at least functional literacy in Hebrew. Assuming that students will not simply tune out and give up, teaching Jewish Studies classes entirely in Hebrew can challenge students to learn content in another language, especially when the focus is not simply acquiring the language itself. Teaching in Hebrew can also create a different learning environment for students, one in which students with better linguistic skills can compete and interact with students who may have better content acquisition skills but not necessarily commensurate Hebrew skills.

Insisting on an all-Hebrew learning environment may also increase the functional vocabulary of students. Learning a language ceases being a passive activity focused on memorizing vocabulary and conjugations, but becomes one in which students must utilize their knowledge in discussions and debates. If students can successfully be held to a demanding standard of Hebrew interaction within the classroom, this can lead to their developing higher linguistic abilities and increasing their capacity to manipulate complex ideas in another language. As a result, even if everyone in the same classroom doesn't master the same degree of Hebrew proficiency, everyone may able to function at a much higher level as a result.

It is also important to note that not all Jewish Studies teachers are themselves fluent in Hebrew. Therefore, the fact that teachers themselves may struggle to find the right word or make occasional mistakes can provide a powerful demonstration of the importance of Hebrew for nonnative speakers. When American Jewish Studies teachers teach in Hebrew, they also serve as role models who are sufficiently committed to the language despite the fact that they may make mistakes themselves in their efforts to teach in Hebrew. Students learn that one doesn't have to be a linguistic scholar in order to open their mouths and try to communicate in public in a language other than their native tongue. When students and teachers struggle together to express their thoughts in imperfect Hebrew, this demonstrates the commitment of Jewish educators to the value and importance of Hebrew in Jewish education.

Similar arguments can be advanced regarding the use of Hebrew versus English translations of religious texts. Even in an English milieu, the study of Biblical or Rabbinic texts in Hebrew can limit the comprehension of the students, slow the pace of study, and require frequent translations of difficult words and phrases. However, the insistence on studying traditional texts in their original language can lead to students building up a functional literary vocabulary and can challenge students to master at least reading and comprehension skills, while also providing a learning environment in which everyone can participate on similar levels, independent of linguistic ability. Students also benefit from learning key words and concepts in their original tongue, which can increase the depth of their understanding.

The use of Hebrew in Jewish education is a defining issue in Jewish Studies today because it can potentially determine the quality of Jewish education students will acquire. It raises the issue of whether a Jewish education in English translation is equivalent to or as effective as a more Hebrew-based education in transmitting Jewish values to future generations. In some settings, instruction in Hebrew may be a formidable obstacle and serve to hinder learning in the classroom. However, a commitment to learning how to speak Hebrew and study Hebrew texts should be a central component of all formats of Jewish education. Even if there is a mixture of Hebrew and English, the demonstration of the commitment to Hebrew literacy is a vital goal of Jewish education. While everyone has his or her own opinions and experiences in this matter, it is vital that Jewish educators be aware of the potential advantages and disadvantages of Hebrew Jewish Studies classes and work to overcome the challenges they represent so as to increase the ability of American Jews to speak and learn in Hebrew.

TRACKING

There is a debate within the world of Jewish education as to how to divide students in Jewish studies classes: whether heterogeneously, with students of high and low academic skills and Hebrew knowledge randomly mixed, or homogeneously, with students of similar academic level and Hebrew knowledge placed together. Most Jewish day schools track students based on their Hebrew skills; but, while there are advantages and disadvantages to both forms of groupings, there are unique advantages that can be achieved only through heterogeneous class divisions.

Homogenous groupings tend to place students who have similar Hebrew skills together. That is, if they can read and translate Hebrew texts at approximately the same level, they are placed in the same Jewish Studies classes. What generally happens is that two levels are created: an upper, "advanced" class and a lower, "intermediate" or "*Mechina*" (preparatory) class. There are, in fact, many advantages to this kind of homogeneous class groupings with trackings based on Hebrew language skills:

- Tracking allows greater in-depth study. Students in a higher level Jewish Studies class are able to cover material more thoroughly and discuss more issues than students at lower levels. Since reading and comprehension of Hebrew is not an insurmountable obstacle for higher level students, teachers can present more texts than can be covered in mixed class groupings or lower levels.

- Tracking allows more sophisticated analysis of Jewish texts. If students who are unable to translate Hebrew texts and discuss them in Hebrew are placed in their own class, the students in the upper level class are able to engage in more mature, complex discussions of the ideas and related concepts. While Hebrew language skills are not always an indication of intellectual maturity, those student who have been able to learn more Hebrew frequently have better study habits than students with less command of Hebrew. Therefore, this can help boost the sophistication of class discussions and studies at higher levels, allowing those students to create a more challenging educational environment for themselves.

- Tracking also enables lower level classes to spend more time on English translations of texts for greater understanding. Often, with heterogeneous grouping, students with weaker Hebrew skills get left behind while the rest of the class progresses. Creating specific sections for these students provides them with more time to comprehend the Hebrew and master the translation. Also, tracking helps students in lower levels actually to learn the content of the texts and then to analyze and examine the content in depth.

- Tracking allows upper level classes to move faster. Higher level students can cover more material at a faster pace than lower classes. Because they understand the material more quickly, they can move on to new texts and topics at a faster rate. As was mentioned previously, students can cover more material without having to spend class time on translation and explanation of texts. In addition, tracking allows lower level classes to move more slowly to ensure that students grasp the material at a pace that is appropriate for them.

- Tracking usually ensures fewer discipline issues at higher levels. Students who have not been able to achieve adequate Hebrew proficiency sometimes are the source of class discipline problems. Higher level classes frequently have fewer classroom management issues because these students tend to be more academically motivated and interested in their studies. Provided that there are sufficient numbers of teachers, lower level sections can be divided into smaller sections to ensure greater attention to the students.

- Tracking enables lower level classes to move at an appropriate pace. Students who are not proficient in Hebrew are often overwhelmed and unable to understand the material they are being unfairly expected to master in higher level classes. Creating lower level classes enables these students to learn the material in a manner and at a rate that allows them to fully learn the texts and ideas.

- Tracking makes it easier for teachers to tailor their material to the appropriate class level. Teachers of higher level classes are able to discard or deal more quickly with "basic" texts and ideas so as to create a curriculum that is customized to more advanced students. Teachers of lower level classes are able to omit or modify overly challenging texts and focus more exclusively on those materials and concepts that will be appropriate to their students. Each class and level learns at a pace and degree of sophistication that is challenging to its students.

Despite the number of these apparent advantages to tracking students in Jewish Studies classes, there are also distinct disadvantages to homogenous class groupings that can negatively affect the education of all the students:

- Tracking creates a social environment of "smart" vs. "dumb" kids. Whenever a school program officially separates students based on certain areas of skill mastery, this automatically raises issues of self-esteem among the students, leading them to differentiate among themselves. Not only does the school separate them into different classes based on their academic abilities, but students label themselves: higher level students assume a certain air of arrogance as they consider themselves among the academic elite of a school, and lower level students begin to think of themselves as less capable. In one "B" level course I taught, students even cheerfully called themselves the "dumb" class. But no matter how sanguine students may be about these labels, schools should not play any role in marginalizing students or reducing their sense of self-esteem.

- Tracking creates unequal knowledge levels among any given grade. For instance, due to the tracking system in my own Jewish high school, students in different levels (A, B, or C sections) taking the exact same course complete each year of Rabbinic Studies having learned different texts at varying degrees of sophistication. It is also difficult for teachers to plan curricula in the next grade level if they are unsure of what students have learned previously. Further, students who advance or drop down to different levels are unprepared for their next level of classes. There being no uniformity to what students are being taught, tracked Jewish Studies classes may be considered "separate but equal."

- Tracking students precludes the possibility of peer tutoring. Much has been written in the world of education about cooperative learning and the advantages of students teaching fellow students. However, in "advanced," "intermediate," or "beginners" classes, there is often not sufficient differentiation among the students' skill levels for stronger students to be able adequately to tutor weaker students. As a result, students are almost entirely dependent upon the teacher to provide help and guidance in their studies.

- Tracking creates a learning environment that is teacher-dependent The learning process remains a teacher-oriented experience if there are reduced opportunities for students of different levels to learn together; therefore, students are unable to develop independent or group learning skills. While it is natural and expected in education in general for students to look to their teachers for help and guidance, it is also important for students to learn how to utilize and share their own unique skills and knowledge with their peers. Tracking students eliminates or at least greatly reduces this possibility.

- Tracking tends to redistribute discipline issues at the lower levels. Clearly this is not always true, but, as noted previously, students who have not been able to achieve adequate Hebrew proficiency sometimes are the source of class discipline problems, due, perhaps, to a range of learning difficulties these students may be experiencing. As a result, lower level Jewish Studies classes tend to have a greater number of students with behavior and even learning difficulties. Tracking thus leads to a form of academic segregation.

- Tracking leads to a lack of depth of study and analysis in lower skill level sections. Although this is not always true, the converse of what was described previously is that students with greater Hebrew proficiency tend to be bright, intellectually curious, and quick learners. Their ability to learn a second language is often indicative of greater academic motivation and interest in learning. Students relegated to lower levels tend to lack the motivation and skills with which to engage in sophisticated textual analysis and discussion. Therefore, teachers of higher skill level sections build on the natural analytical skills of their students, while teachers of lower skill sections often must work to achieve simple mastery of the material, leaving little time for or energy for higher level, more sophisticated analysis of the material.

- Tracking tends to slow the pace of learning in lower levels, which in turn compounds issues of self-esteem among the students. As a result of customized curricula for lower levels, teachers tend to teach fewer texts and at a slower pace. This, in turn, undermines the confidence and self-image of these students when they compare their classes with upper level classes. While a slower pace may assure that students in lower levels understand the material, it may also lead them to become frustrated with the reduced rate of covering new material. Such frustration can sap students' motivation and lead to classroom discipline problems. While a slower pace may be a godsend to academically challenged students, tracking is no assurance that they will not feel that such a slow pace is indicative of their cognitive skills. In other words, even if they benefit from the pace, they may internalize their resentment of not being able to keep up with the pace in another section.

- Tracking undermines the building of a sense of community among a grade or even in an entire school. Academic segregation tends to weaken and impair the creation of a strong sense of community among students because there is no sense of having shared intellectual experiences. Taking the same courses as previous generations of students or grades can often lead to the creation of a student culture that glorifies the common academic hardships they have all endured and survived together. However, when students experience vastly different courses of study, they are deprived of this sense of everyone having shared the same thing. Teenagers, who are particularly class conscious as a part of their maturation process, tend to accentuate such differences, which can weaken the development of a sense of cohesiveness and unity among students.

- Tracking unintentionally fosters self-centered values in higher skill level sections. An unintended and even deleterious result of tracking is that it is perceived by students as a means to enable "smart" kids to study more challenging subjects faster by removing the "dumb" kids. Students in "advanced" levels absorb these subconscious values, which may lead to the glorification of individual academic excellence to the detriment of the progress and learning of the group or grade as a whole. In other words, despite the fact that this is not its purpose, tracking can foster intellectual egocentrism among the advanced sections while also, as was mentioned previously, hindering the development of a healthy sense of self-esteem among students in lower skill level sections.

Heterogeneous divisions, the random or even distribution of students with diverse text skills and knowledge of Hebrew, is another way to approach the instruction of Jewish Studies. In contrast with homogenous groupings, no distinctions are made in the division of students into classes; or different skill levels are taken into account precisely to create balanced class sections. There are both disadvantages and advantages to this distribution method. However, in my opinion, the benefits of heterogeneous grouping outweigh its failings. In addition, the values that are consciously cultivated make it a superior means of working to concretize a number of Jewish values.

Before detailing the advantages of dividing classes into heterogeneous skill level sections, it is important and instructive to note the failings of this approach:

- Heterogeneous grouping limits the depth of study. With a mixture of students of a variety of different Hebrew skill levels, teachers must assure that all students understand as much of the material as possible; thus they must limit the number of subjects and concepts that can be discussed. Also, heterogeneous grouping limits the number of interesting tangents and digressions that can be pursued without confusing or losing the students. The unity and overall pace of a class may sometimes be slowed, and the texts and topics covered may be limited.

- Heterogeneous classes limit the sophistication of the analysis of texts and ideas. Not all students are prepared for or capable of discussing complex, subtle concepts at the same time. As was mentioned previously concerning the merits of tracking, with mixed groups, teachers must limit the intricacy and difficulty in their curricula as they strive for intellectual parity in classes that enroll students with a diversity of skill levels.

- Heterogeneous classes cannot guarantee that some students will not be left behind. Even with teachers striving for academic inclusiveness, some students will still not be able to function at a level that will ensure their academic success even in a mixed class. Despite the advantages of mixed groupings (see further on in this chapter), they cannot guarantee academic success.

- Heterogeneous classes also make it difficult for teachers to enable all students to achieve high rates of academic success. Despite the best efforts, it is always a struggle for even the most talented teachers successfully to ensure that all students feel included in the class and are making progress. In order to work with so many students at different skill levels, teachers must split their time among these different constituencies, which may lead to a lack of focus in the class in general.

Having acknowledged these limitations, the advantages of heterogeneous classes outweigh these concerns for the following reasons:

- Heterogeneous classes preclude labeling of students, externally or internally. Because all of the students are mixed evenly or randomly, there are no "smart" classes or "dumb" classes. Individual students are not labeled or encouraged to think of themselves as either "advanced" or "beginner." All of the students have the opportunity to consider themselves as being academically equal as they participate equally in the same classes. The only differences among students are those that emerge naturally and inevitably as individual students begin to excel and succeed in different classes and subjects.

- Heterogeneous classes enable students to tutor one another. Having many different levels of students in one class allows students to help each other, working together in *havruta* (cooperative study groups). Students are given the opportunity to teach as well as learn in the same classroom, thereby increasing their overall academic proficiency.

- Heterogeneous classes help build patience and tolerance among students with different skill and knowledge levels. While working together with many, varied skill levels may be occasionally frustrating to teacher and students alike, the value of continuing to learn in this kind of environment is that students, and even teachers, must develop patience and work to ensure that everyone advances and understands the material. These are valuable skills as well as Jewish values, which should be developed in a Jewish classroom as they help to instill the skills necessary to work for and achieve unity and cohesiveness in the Jewish community.

- Heterogeneous classes are more independent of the teacher, and teachers can formally and informally empower students to teach each other. While high level students may naturally be able to teach and explain different concepts or texts, lower level students benefit through the exposure to fellow students as role models. Repetition and the demonstration of the mastery of knowledge become integral elements of the learning process in such a classroom. Cooperative learning is a powerful element in the repertoire of teaching modes that should be used in any classroom, for the more approaches and ways there are for students to absorb information, the greater are the chances that any one or a number of them will prove successful with different students.

- In heterogeneous classes, discipline issues are spread evenly, or at least randomly, through class sections. Rather than intentionally grouping learning-challenged children or students with histories of misbehavior in one section, random or mixed grouping allows these students to be "diluted" among the class sections, thereby reducing their ability to sabotage classroom management and placing them in a class that will potentially provide them with more appropriate, disciplined student role models.

- Heterogeneous classes build a sense of communal spirit and unity within a grade or an entire school. When students of varied Hebrew proficiency have no choice but to work together, despite any social and academic frustrations that may arise, this can provide them with the opportunity to realize through such experiences that they must work together as a community if they are to succeed. As the saying goes, a chain is only as strong as its weakest link. However, when all members of a class, the other links in a chain, are motivated to help strengthen the "weaker" students, the overall quality of education in the class is improved for everyone. The emotional intelligence skills that are built up through such experiences are just as important, if not more so, as the intellectual, academic skills, especially from the standpoint of the Jewish tradition that emphasizes the need for people to support and care for one another.

- Heterogeneous classes help foster a sense of generosity as students must work with different levels of students. The nature of mixed classes requires that different students work with each other in a variety of work group situations. The very activity of continuously working together can serve to create a sense of giving and helpfulness as students realize that they are capable of assisting their friends and classmates. There is no better way to demonstrate the value of *hesed,* kindness, than through living and acting on this value every day in class.

- Heterogeneous classes demonstrate that the pursuit of pure, individual academic excellence is not necessarily a (Jewish) value. If the classes throughout the school are structured in a balanced way, meaning a mix of heterogeneous and homogenous classes, this can help prevent students from developing the idea that their classes have been arranged so as separate those who "can't succeed" from those who can. Students will not necessarily label themselves as "smart" and "dumb" provided that they are mixed in heterogeneous classes throughout each day.

- Heterogeneous classes are easier for teachers because they only have to plan one curriculum for all students. Teachers don't have to create a variety of different lesson plans or curricula for similar classes, and such uniformity can make it easier for different teachers (and students) to continue learning at the next grade level or subject matter.

- Heterogeneous classes foster a commitment to the ideals of intellectual pluralism and tolerance. Even though we live in a stratified society, the Jewish tradition insists that we view every human being as holy, having been created in the image of God. Despite intellectual differences, students at the earliest ages must learn to function and succeed in a heterogeneous society and, indeed, to value the very heterogeneity of that society. Homogenous classes can create false expectations among students about what life holds in store for them and should hold in store for them. However, there should be no limits to what students aspire to, nor should other students expect that they are on life's "fast track." Class divisions should not segregate students based on academic differences, for this only ingrains in students the idea that this is the way things should be. Because of the primacy of justice in the Jewish tradition, it is incumbent upon educators to encourage a commitment to intellectual egalitarianism. Rather than mirror the stratification of society, Jewish schools can and should strive for more—namely, to transform society to better reflect our ideals as Jews.

Given the fact that there are advantages and disadvantages to each division, it is important to balance homogeneously grouped classes with heterogeneously grouped classes within an educational setting. For example, in a day school setting, Social Studies and English could be heterogeneously mixed, Math and Sciences homogeneously mixed (based on quantitative math and science skills), but Jewish Studies classes should be heterogeneously mixed for all of the reasons stated previously. In non-day-school settings, heterogeneous class divisions are by no means perfect; however, they are they best way to teach the greatest number of students Jewish Studies and to work to fulfill significant Jewish values in our communities.

Navigation Skills

I once announced to a class that we were going to study some selections from *Pirkei Avot* (a volume of the *Mishnah* dealing with ethical statements of the early Rabbis). A student then said, "I've heard about *Pirkei Avot* and even studied some of it before, but I have no idea what it is or where it is. So what is it and where does it come from?" This question indicates a significant gap in many Jewish Studies classes. Namely, students need to know where they are in a given text, book, genre of literature, and subject in order to make sense of it. For instance, many Jews, young people and adults alike, do not know what the difference is between the *Gemara* and the Talmud—or if there is one. (They are used as synonyms; however, the *Gemara* is just a part of the Talmud, which also contains the *Mishnah*). What is *Midrash* and how does one go about looking for stories about different topics? Where does one look to study original Rabbinic sources about *Kashrut*? Whether a course of Jewish Studies follows a text-based or topic-based curriculum, students must be able to "navigate" their way through all of the major genres and works of Rabbinic literature as well as the books of the Bible.

Regrettably, a common experience among many Jewish students—as my student's comment indicated—is the sense of being "lost" when it comes to Jewish Studies. Students may be studying a story, a set of laws, or a prophecy from the Bible, but they have no idea where it is located in the Bible. They may know what book of the Bible they are studying but not know where it appears in the order of other books or what the other books are. This is especially true when it comes to the study of Rabbinic literature. The *Mishnah* and *Gemara* are often referred to as the "sea of Talmud"; however, many students feel that they are adrift on this ocean with no sense of where they are or where they are going.

Because of this, it is vital that a significant component of all Jewish text courses should include background "navigation" information, which helps establish the historical and literary place of the texts being studied. All Bible classes should include a short unit on the structure of the Bible. Students should learn the three main divisions of the Bible (*Torah, Neviim, Ketuvim*) as well as their constituent books. Students should also learn the basic historical context of the Bible and be familiar with key events in Israelite history. Simply framing the study of Biblical texts could go a long way toward dispelling the sense of unfamiliarity with the Bible that many students experience. It is not my intention to go into the details of this information; rather, I shall highlight some of the major "landmarks" when it comes to providing students with a "map" to understanding Jewish Studies courses.

Because the study of Rabbinic texts is so vast, it is not always feasible to include a complete background of Rabbinic literature and history in the study of any given Rabbinic text. However, the study of specific kinds of Rabbinic texts should include background information pertinent to the study of those particular texts. For instance, truly to understand and appreciate the *Mishnah,* students should have an understanding of the centrality of the Second Temple in ancient Jewish life and the national trauma that occurred as a result of its destruction in 70 C.E. This then provides the context to understand the work of the *Tannaim,* the Rabbis who created and formulated the early Rabbinic oral traditions, as well as the accomplishment of Rebbi Yehudah HaNasi, the editor of the *Mishnah.* Students should learn the names and general contents of the six *Sedarim* (orders) of the *Mishnah* as well as the names and general contents of specific tractates under discussion. Not only will the study of the *Sedarim* and tractates help students learn the literary structure of the *Mishnah* (and the rest of the Talmud), but it will also provide them with a basis for understanding the Rabbinic reformulation of Judaism as it developed and grew from its Biblical roots.

Once students understand the world of the *Mishnah,* they have a basis for learning about the development of the *Gemara* and Midrashic literature. Students should learn about the limitations of the terse, decisive literary style of the *Mishnah* before studying how the *Amoraim* labored to re-expand Jewish law to include full discussions and arguments about the underlying legal and moral principles of the *Mishnah.*

The study of *Midrash* is often even more confusing than the study of *Mishnah* or *Gemara* because of the diversity of literary genres. Therefore, it can be helpful for students to learn the basic differences between *Halakhah* (Jewish law) and *Aggadah* (imaginative literature) as well as the role of *Midrash* (the process of interpretation and explanation of texts in addition to the texts themselves). Once they have grasped the nuances between *Midrash Halakhah* and *Midrash Aggadah,* students should learn the characteristics of the three main literary genres of *Aggadah,* namely, exegetical (explanatory), homiletical (moral and ethical), and narrative (storytelling).

Similarly, the study of Jewish codes of law is not as straightforward as it might seem. Because of the profusion of different Jewish legal codes in different periods of Jewish history, students should learn about the authors and literary goals of several major codes, such as the Rambam (Rabbi Moses ben Maimon, also known as Maimonides), who wrote the *Mishneh Torah,* Rabbi Ya'acov Asher, who wrote the *Arba'ah Turim* (known simply as the *Tur*), and Rabbis Joseph Karo and Moshe Isserles, the authors of the *Shulkhan Arukh*. Students should also learn the various structures and outlines of these codes so that they can become capable of finding and learning information on their own.

No matter what texts are taught, it is important that students be given the tools to "navigate" in that type of literature. Just as a driver should know how to read a map and be familiar with the general topography of a particular area where they intend to travel, students of Jewish texts should be generally familiar with the various "terrains" of Jewish literature, Biblical and Rabbinic, and know how to go about finding what they want to know.

Using Technology in Jewish Studies

The current challenge for all educators is how best to utilize the latest technology in computers and the internet in the classroom. Although it is nearly impossible to consider all possible uses, the availability of tremendous numbers of Jewish texts in CD-ROM format and the accessibility of nearly every Jewish organization via e-mail or the World Wide Web, are tremendous assets for advanced study and in-depth, interactive research projects. Because the amount of relevant Jewish Studies information available via computers increases constantly, the following suggestions are some of the most simple, reliable, easy-to-incorporate uses of these technologies. Here are some ideas for educators to bear in mind as they plan their curricula.

Compact Discs in a Read Only Memory (CD-ROM) format are able to store enormous amounts of information, encompassing the capacity of a small library of Jewish texts. There are numerous computer software companies and other organizations that are storing more and more Jewish texts on CD-ROMs. One of the chief advantages of having access to this kind of information in this format is the ability to search and locate exact quotes, key words, and ideas throughout the Bible and Rabbinic literature. For teachers, the ability quickly to track down every quote that Rabbi Yochanon ben Broka (a minor rabbi from the period of the Mishnah) ever said can be profoundly useful. Using the search engines available in nearly all of the CD-ROMs, it is possible to determine with absolute certainty how many times the word "slave" appears in the Bible (261 times), every usage of the hermeneutical principle of "*Kal V'Homer*" (an argument *a fortiori*) that appears in the Talmud (790 times), or every instance throughout Midrashic literature where the Rabbis quoted from Genesis 1:28, "Be fruitful and multiply" (44 times). Using these CD-ROMs, which now have nearly every major classic Jewish text on them, from the Torah to the *Zohar*, both in Hebrew and English, educators no longer have to rely on half-remembered quotes or incomplete and inaccurate indices and concordances. All of the information is available through a keyboard and computer.

Another major advantage of using the CD-ROM technology is the ability to customize text study sheets. Without the use of computers, teachers must copy a printed text and then cut and paste the selections on a separate sheet of paper. However, using CD-ROMs, it is possible to select exactly and only the quotes that a teacher wants to use and then electronically "paste" these selections into a new computer document and print a clean, precise, and exact textual study sheet. This avoids the waste of copying, throwing away scraps of paper, and filling up a school's *geniza* (special disposal of holy texts) with discarded holy texts. A further benefit is that the Hebrew quotes can be altered so as to replace God's name with Hebrew replacements, such as the Hebrew letter "hey," which then obviates the need to place the text study sheet in a *geniza* after use. In this way, teachers can customize their study sheets and arrange texts in any way they choose on a sheet.

Students can use CD-ROM technology in the same way that teachers use it, such as creating text study sheets for their classes and tracking down sources and quotes. Much of Jewish text study is self-referential; in other words, Biblical prophets and other figures often quote earlier sections of the Bible. Teachers should bear in mind that, using CD-ROMs, students can be assigned the task of locating these quotes in their original Biblical books. Similarly, the *Gemara* often quotes the *Mishnah,* and *Midrashim* often quote Biblical verses and other statements from the Talmud. Homework for students can and should begin to include the responsibility of using CD-ROMs to locate these sources so that they can study the original context of sources. What used to take hours of pouring through scholarly indices and concordances can now be reduced to minutes of computer time.

Even the classic Jewish reference, the *Encyclopedia Judaica,* a seventeen-volume work (published in 1973 by Keter Publishing House), has been put into CD-ROM format. Research projects that previously required extensive use of the index volume and then the painstaking search through numerous entries and multiple volumes can now be accomplished with a few clicks on a computer mouse. While the *EJ* has been enhanced in its CD-ROM format with film clips, sound files with the Hebrew pronunciation of names, and examples of music, the most powerful and important tool that has been added is the hyperlinking of related entries. In other words, while reading one entry, it is possible to click a key word or idea in that entry and move directly to the article on that key word. Teachers should try to incorporate the use of these tools into Jewish Studies not simply to learn the use of this technology, but because these tools are more efficient and can truly save students time and energy.

The use and access to the internet, e-mail, and the World Wide Web (WWW) have assumed great prominence in the world of computing today. In fact, most people think of the internet, the global network of linked computers, as being synonymous with the WWW. The most easily accessible aspect of the internet, however, is electronic mail. Despite the bewildering potential number of uses of the internet, the following are some of the most basic ways in which teachers and students can take advantage of this new technology.

The idea that the Jewish people are unified throughout time and space takes on new meaning in the cyber age. Using e-mail, Jewish students can now link up with and become "net-pals" or "cyber-pals" with other Jewish students around the world. Students and classes in the United States can communicate with students in Russia or Israel or Australia as easily as they can correspond with their friends across town. E-mail can provide a tangible demonstration of the unity of the Jewish people.

Using the World Wide Web, teachers and students alike can access the card catalogs and holdings of numerous libraries across the country and around the world. Sometimes, learning the titles and general content of books can help teachers and students determine the direction of a research assignment and project. In addition, many magazines, periodicals, and papers also publish either partial or full versions of their articles on-line, allowing public access to their holdings. The potential for research, especially for Jewish projects, is tremendous.

In addition, many Jewish organizations, universities, businesses, and individuals are represented on the WWW. Teachers and students alike can contact people directly as resources in research projects. Depending upon the organization, Web pages often contain a wealth of information or have hyperlinks directly to other related organizations. Using the WWW and e-mail, it is now much easier to get in touch directly with people who can be helpful in the creation of curricula and research projects.

Finally, it is possible to "publish" the results of student or class research projects on the WWW. Many schools with access to the WWW also have the capacity to create and post their own Web pages. It can be a terrific source of pride and accomplishment for students to publish their own material in the public domain. Web technology allows students to post the text of research papers, scan photos, attach sound files, and create hyperlinks to other related Web pages as part of their multimedia presentations.

It is beyond the scope of this chapter to list all of the possible uses of computers and the internet in the classroom; however, there are basic ways that educators can begin to utilize this technology for Jewish Studies. Using relatively simple and easily accessible CD-ROM-capable computers, e-mail, and Web browsers, Jewish educators can create challenging and compelling projects. While computer technology may not be the educational panacea that many people believe it to be, making use of the current resources can greatly aid and enhance the ability of educators and students to increase their Jewish literacy.

FORMATS OF JEWISH EDUCATION

What is the most effective format in which to provide Jewish education? In other words, what kind of school has the greatest chance of success in instilling a love of Jewish learning and a passion for Jewish life in students? The answers depend upon the age of the students and the quality of the Jewish educators. It is obvious that, based on the time alone that is allocated for Jewish studies, (non-Orthodox) Jewish day schools have more time and greater continuity in terms of daily contact with which to immerse children in Jewish learning. Yet, each setting for Jewish education, whether it be a full-time denominational Jewish day school, a communal Jewish day school, a synagogue religious school, or a supplemental Hebrew high school, has its own unique strengths and weaknesses.

Jewish Day Schools: Denominational and Communal

Why have non-Orthodox full-day Jewish schools? Although the Orthodox Jewish community is relatively tiny in the United States in comparison to the Jewish Renewal, Reform, Reconstructionist, and Conservative movements, the Orthodox communities recognized very early on in the American experience that only a complete and all-embracing Orthodox Jewish educational system could come close to guaranteeing that their future generations would emerge as Jewishly Orthodox adults. Because of the ever-present temptations of American secular life, the Orthodox communities feared that each succeeding generation would inevitably "drift" to the "left," that is, become slightly more liberal, less observant, and less faithful than the previous generation. Therefore, to counteract this drift, long ago many Orthodox day and high schools consciously adopted a more rigid, more observant, more dogmatic approach to Jewish life and learning than the very communities that established them. The intent was that even if the students of these Orthodox schools ended up growing less observant and theologically rigorous than their educational background, they would still remain squarely within the realm of the Orthodox community albeit with somewhat relaxed standards of observance and belief.

While this conscious attempt to counteract the drift towards religious liberalism may have been successful in maintaining a steady course in the earliest stages of Orthodox education in this country, such schools and their communities are now reaping the results of their own success. Rather than counteracting a drift to the left, many Orthodox schools have, instead, produced even more rigid, more scrupulously observant, and more dogmatic Jews than ever before. Many such schools successfully counteracted this feared drift and graduated young Jews who were entirely as scrupulous and dogmatic in their approach to Jewish life as their schools. As a result, many Orthodox schools have themselves become even more dogmatic than before, creating entire Jewish communities that are becoming ever more intolerant of liberal Jews, pluralism, and religious tolerance. Thus, many traditional families in the Reform and Conservative movements no longer feel comfortable sending their children to schools that institutionally devalue them as Jews and their denominations as legitimate religious Jewish communities.

Rather than silently acquiescing to such religious alienation, serious, committed liberal Jews have begun to accept the new challenges of graduating practicing and knowledgeable Jews by founding full-day non-Orthodox Jewish schools. Instead of accepting as inevitable the current demographic trends that indicate greater assimilation and alienation among liberal Jews, liberal American Jews have sought to create comprehensive institutions of Jewish learning that will successfully train Jewish children and teenagers to enter adult life as both fully integrated American citizens and knowledgeable, practicing Jews.

Full-time non-Orthodox Jewish day schools, especially those associated with a particular denomination of American Judaism, are perhaps the single most effective format for Jewish education for a number of reasons. The first is that Reform and Conservative Jewish day schools offer courses in Bible, Rabbinics, Jewish History, and Hebrew classes that are completely integrated with general studies classes such as English, Social Studies, Math, Science, Art, and Gym. This is significant because it communicates the message that Jewish subjects are just as significant and important as general studies classes. And this fact by itself creates a model of a fully integrated American and Jewish identity. Jewish learning then is not placed in direct competition with after-school and evening music lessons, sports, and socializing. Jewish Studies are a complete part of a student's educational identity. The Jewish day schools, a single school with a single faculty consisting of both Jewish and general studies teachers, are models for students in terms of intellectual and social integration.

In addition, a full-day Jewish school engages students in Jewish learning during their peak hours of concentration and focus. It is very difficult to absorb information when one is tired, such as at the end of a day or during the evening hours. The classroom discussions in Jewish classes in a full-day Jewish school are filled with high energy, laughter, thinking, and incisive debate, which are much easier to achieve when Jewish classes are part-and-parcel of a full-day school. Jewish day schools are able to teach Jewish subjects at a level and depth that other non-day Jewish schools obviously cannot due to time constraints precisely at a time when students are best able to absorb the information. They provide an environment more conducive to the permanent acquisition of Jewish values and learning. Learning of any kind is a long-term process. The more one is immersed in a learning environment, the more effective and long-lasting the lessons. Simply put, the more time students spend studying Jewish subjects, the more likely it is that such information will occupy more of their thoughts and influence the development of their identities. Full-day Jewish schools provide a holistic approach to Jewish and general education and expose students to a more consistent and intensive Jewish environment expressly designed for their complete educational growth.

Jewish day schools can also assign Jewish homework projects as time-consuming and intensive as any English, Math, or Social Studies project. The value of homework is not just that students are obligated to study a topic in greater depth than is possible in class, but that students must make the time on their own to complete assignments. Doing homework instills the value of self-motivation. Because Jewish living and learning is a purely voluntary component of modern American life, Jewish homework assignments can influence Jewish students to make the time to lead Jewish lives and continue the challenge of Jewish learning as adults. If the goal of Jewish education is to encourage observance of Jewish laws and rituals, then the skills that students must acquire in order to function in an academic environment can be easily transferred to Jewish life skills later on in life. For example, observing Shabbat often requires advance preparation of meals and reading Torah for a synagogue requires a great deal of time and practice. If students learn how to discipline themselves regarding Jewish studies as children and young adults, they will be able to apply these same skills to living Jewish lives.

Also, Jewish day schools have the natural advantage of immersing Jewish students in an environment of Jewish living and learning for a majority of the day. The intensity of regular school with all Jewish students, coupled with the environment of Jewish classes and prayer, helps to reinforce the very values and messages that they are learning in the classroom about the importance of Jewish community. Every Jewish schooling experience involves the creation of a mini-Jewish community, no matter how temporary. Children and teenagers learn the bulk of their socialization skills in school throughout the day, whether formally in a classroom or informally through interacting with their peers. Learning to function in a Jewish day school community prepares students to thrive in a Jewish community in the adult world. In addition, in a full-day Jewish school, students and faculty intermix throughout the entire day, praying together in a morning *minyon* as well as in class, in the halls, in the lunchroom, and in extracurricular activities. Barriers between formal and informal education are practically nonexistent in a full-day Jewish school. Faculty interact with students as Jewish role models, as teachers, and as continuously learning Jewish adults throughout the entire day. This further helps students to integrate the values of the Jewish tradition with the civic virtues and knowledge of American life.

Jewish day schools tend to be more successful in transmitting Jewish values and practices because Jewish day schools generally hire full-time teachers at full-time educational wages. This doesn't necessarily guarantee that full-day Jewish schools will always end up employing more qualified teachers than do other formats of Jewish schools, but it does increase the likelihood that a larger number of professional Jewish educators who have chosen to make their living in Jewish education will be attracted to such a school. This often translates into a higher level of professionalism of the faculty, which can only improve the quality of education in the school. It is also more difficult to hide incompetence among the teaching staff in a full-day school than it is in supplemental or synagogue religious schools whose total classroom hours in a week may be less than the those of one day in a full-day Jewish school. Of course, none of these factors guarantees quality among any faculty in any given Jewish day school, but they do increase the level of professional review and standards in such schools. The more professional the faculty, the higher the level of education the students benefit from. This also applies to the quality and level of the Jewish subjects being taught. Better teachers often translates into better educated, more motivated students—and Jews.

Finally, day schools associated with a particular movement, as well as synagogue religious schools, tend to be more successful because they are usually more theologically and ideologically resolved in their educational approach than are other kinds of schools. The old adage, of "two Jews, three opinions" is often played out in sometimes rancorous fashion in the world of Jewish education. However, when school boards, involved laity, Jewish professionals, administrators, and teachers have the advantage of belonging to the same movement they can at least rely on a fairly consistent and institutional approach to Jewish life as articulated by their movement. The Reform, Reconstructionist, and Conservative movements have developed elaborate and detailed approaches to Jewish observance consistent with their philosophies and theology that can be important assets for movement Jewish day schools. While this cannot guarantee success, it can help day schools and synagogue religious schools avoid the pitfalls of other kinds of Jewish schools by beginning discussions of religious education from the same denominational starting point.

After full-time Jewish day schools associated with a particular denomination of American Judaism, community Jewish
day schools are perhaps the next most effective format for
Jewish education. They share nearly all of the advantages
associated with day schools of a particular movement as mentioned previously, such as the integration of subjects, teaching
at peak performance hours, the ability to assign homework,
immersion in a Jewish environment, and a full-time faculty.
However, they are inherently unstable because all communal
Jewish day schools must confront a permanent controversy
not faced by schools associated with a particular denomination: how Jewish should they be, and what kind of Judaism
(that is, "who's Judaism") should be taught or practiced?

Jewish communal day schools are usually founded by
communities because they do not have the finances or a supply of children sufficient to create their own individual movement-based Jewish day schools. Various elements of the Jewish
community pool their resources to procure a site and hire
teachers and administrators. As a result, the official Jewish
curriculum and ritual practices of the school are often carefully crafted compromises intended to appease every constituent of the Jewish community while pleasing no one. One
important constituency that is often attracted to communal
Jewish day schools are secular Jews, who, while they want to
be affiliated with the larger Jewish community, are opposed to
the ritually and theologically oriented religious basis of this
affiliation. The issue of teaching "too much" Judaism and creating and enforcing policies that are "too Jewish" are explosive subjects to these Jews. On the other side, families that are
religiously active in their synagogues often look to the Jewish
communal day schools to prepare their children for their *Bar*
and *Bat Mitzvah* ceremonies, teach them to read and speak
Hebrew, and prepare them to lead more observant lives. Such
goals are not always shared by the secular Jewish families.

Therefore, Jewish communal day schools can range from
those taking their Jewish identity seriously, teaching complex
and demanding Jewish studies curricula, to those that are not
all that Jewish and produce graduates barely literate in
Hebrew or knowledgeable about Jewish holidays and rituals.
Yet, despite these potential disadvantages, Jewish communal

day schools do offer most of the major advantages of full-time denominational Jewish schools.

Synagogue Religious Schools

In the absence of full-time Jewish day schools, whether movement-based or communal, synagogue religious schools (often called "Hebrew schools") are important institutions of Jewish education. In fact, most synagogues offer Hebrew school for the children of members to teach them the basics of Jewish life and observance as well as prepare them for their *Bar* and *Bat Mitzvah* ceremonies. Depending on the affiliation of the synagogue, nearly all Hebrew schools adhere to the educational standards promulgated by their movement. Such standards are usually sufficiently defined to provide an educational framework for religious schools, yet loose enough to enable each synagogue to structure its school so as best to meet the needs of its membership. Despite the ubiquitous nature of synagogue religious schools, they face many challenges.

The most significant challenge confronting Hebrew schools is the fact that they lack precisely the advantages that full-day religious schools enjoy. Hebrew schools are one-subject schools, which have limited time and resources to achieve their goals. Because Hebrew schools meet only on the weekends or in the afternoons or evenings, they are not perceived by the students as "real" school. They are separate, "ersatz" schools that cannot compete with public or private secular schools in terms of the ability to deal with issues of classroom discipline or the seriousness with which their students view their subjects. Hebrew schools are "ersatz" in that they are structured like public schools, with separate classes, classrooms, teachers, and curricular materials. However, because the grades that students earn in religious school have no currency beyond the walls of the synagogue, teachers and administrators have limited means to encourage appropriate behavior or serious learning. One of the chief goals of education beyond the synagogue is to achieve good grades; however, this approach to education falls short when it is applied to synagogue schools. The tools of one educational format do not necessarily translate into other settings.

Synagogue religious schools are also limited in the amount of time they have to educate their students. They can only function during the times and hours that children and families are available and parents are willing to bring their children to the synagogue. Therefore, Hebrew school classes are taught at "off-peak" hours in terms of when students are able to and interested in learning. Late afternoons, early evenings, and even weekends are "down" times for children who attend public schools. Having spent the greater part of their time and energy learning in their regular schools, students are not emotionally primed to focus intellectually outside of the school environment. The fact that Hebrew schools may or may not assign homework only compounds this problem. The subjects and depth of the classes are also all too often overly dependent upon the quality of the teachers employed by the Hebrew school. Unfortunately, the availability and quality of Hebrew school teachers vary greatly from community to community and from synagogue to synagogue. Thus, Hebrew school education is far from consistent. Nevertheless, they are the most common format of Jewish education in the non-Orthodox Jewish world in this country.

However, synagogue religious schools do possess a number of potential educational advantages and assets. The first is that they are fully integrated into the religious lives of the synagogue membership. In other words, attending Hebrew school is often seen as important as, or similar to, synagogue attendance, both to the children and parents alike. Because both the synagogue sanctuary and the classrooms are located in the same building or complex, families tend to view religious school as equivalent to other religious activities. This is positive in that children associate their religious studies as being directly related to living Jewish lives.

Another advantage of Hebrew schools is that they have the potential to include the entire family in the educational process and setting. Family education, that is, classes or experiences designed for adults and children, has become popular in Jewish education because it seeks to influence not just the children or the adults separately, but to help the entire family become religiously competent and confident together. While Jewish day schools obviously seek parental involvement and support, a day school is not an institution that involves the entire family and is not organized (or viewed) as an organization dedicated to communal or family spiritual growth. The greatest advantage of synagogue religious schools is this potential to integrate Jewish learning into the religious life of a family. However, while there are many successful synagogue religious schools, they are beset with many challenges that they must overcome in order to achieve their potential.

Supplemental Jewish Schools

Supplemental Jewish schools (usually Hebrew high schools for teenagers) are another setting for providing young adult Jews with a Jewish education. However, Hebrew high schools are beset by their own unique challenges. Successful Hebrew high schools offer four advantages over synagogue religious schools. Freed from having to train students for *Bar* or *Bat Mitzvah,* they can offer classes on many different, even exotic topics that prove of greater interest to teenagers. In addition, they have the ability to teach these topics in greater depth than do religious schools because teenagers are more intellectually capable than are pre-*Bar* and *Bat Mitzvah* students. Also, the students who attend Hebrew high school programs do so voluntarily as attendance is not mandatory as it is for many synagogue religious school students, who are required to attend in preparation for their Bar and Bat Mitzvah ceremonies. And, finally, many teenagers are attracted to Hebrew high schools by the excitement of socializing with their friends in a Jewish environment.

While there are many successful Hebrew high school programs, they are nevertheless limited by many of the same challenges facing synagogue religious schools. Hebrew high school classes are offered either during weekday evenings or on Sundays, times that are not the most conducive to serious Jewish learning. Also, the very attraction of socializing with their peers can prove too great a distraction to teenagers and limit the effectiveness of these programs. Thus, the educational advantages of many Hebrew high schools have been eclipsed by the socializing of their students. The pursuit of social relationships has become the primary focus of many students.

Further, the amount of time in which students attend Hebrew high school classes is simply insufficient to provide Jewish teenagers with the Jewish skills and knowledge they will need to continue their Jewish lives at college or afterwards in their adult lives. A few hours of Jewish studies a week is inadequate to equip young adult Jews with a broad, sophisticated, in-depth, and practical knowledge of Jewish observance, text study, Jewish history, and theology, which they need to help them establish firm Jewish identities. College life is infinitely appealing and attractive to young adults; therefore, Jewish teens need all of the practical and theoretical Jewish knowledge they can possibly acquire to feel religiously self-confident and competent on a university campus. Hebrew high schools, despite their unique appeals and advantages, are not sufficient by themselves to provide this information.

In short, there is a great dichotomy between the expectation that public or private high schools will train Jewish children and teenagers to be well-rounded, informed American citizens and the expectation that synagogue religious schools or supplemental Hebrew high schools can bridge the gap and teach them to be knowledgeable, practicing Jews as well. When communal and educational paradigms change and the landscape of Jewish education begins to shift, as older, once universally accepted values and institutions find themselves competing with newer, more controversial values and institutions, it is only natural that there is going to be tension between different constituencies in the world of Jewish education. Supplemental Jewish schools are competing more and more with Jewish day schools for students and community support. It is hoped that, through the careful study and comparison of all formats of Jewish education, the light created from such a tension will outshine the heat of the moment and lead to the improvement and continuity of the American Jewish community in the long run.

Afterword

I believe that being a Jewish educator is the single most important and significant profession in the Jewish community at this time. Jewish teachers have the opportunity to directly impact the life of a child or young adult more than any other person in his or her life—sometimes including the parents. What Jewish teachers teach and how they do it can affect the depth and quality of children's Jewish life as they mature and grow into adults. It can affect who they will socialize with, date, and marry; it can affect what they eat, how they will spend their time, and even how they will conceive of their personal relationship with God.

A strong, effective, and wise Jewish teacher can have a profoundly positive impact on a young person's life, improving the very experiences of living his or her entire life. Conversely, a poor, ill-equipped Jewish teacher can ruin a child's experience with Judaism, inhibiting personal spiritual growth, demanding dogmatic acceptance of various ideas and beliefs, using inappropriate threats to force or guarantee observance of Jewish rituals, and teaching material that is either so obscure or so narrowly focused as to convey an erroneous impression of Judaism. Therefore, the quality of Jewish education can and should be the focus of ongoing monitoring and improvement.

Jewish continuity—the obligation of the Jewish people to endure and thrive as a unique and distinct religious people—means little if the members of the Jewish community are not sufficiently educated to understand the significance of their religious heritage. Some people argue that Jewish education is one of the most effective means to combat the alienation, assimilation, intermarriage, and ignorance that are affecting the Jewish communities of North America—even if this education is mediocre. But why settle for mediocrity when excellence is within our reach? Why settle for Jewish education as a mere "answer" to the challenges of Jewish continuity when it has the potential to address so much more?

I happened upon Jewish education by accident. As a newly ordained rabbi without any idea of what I wanted to do, I found myself teaching Jewish Studies in a communal Jewish day school. After surviving the normal and natural range of emotions that all new teachers experience their first year, ranging from feelings of terror, panic, inadequacy, and hostility, I discovered that not only did I like teaching—I loved teaching! As I have pursued my career in education and the pulpit, my commitment to Jewish education remains the focus of my professional and personal endeavors. And even as I have affected the course of the Jewish lives of my students, I have become transformed myself by my own experiences as a teacher. Not only have I continued to learn more in the process of my pedagogical preparations, but I have also grown spiritually through my contact with my students of all ages—children, teenagers, young adults, and mature adults. In short, Jewish education has the power to transform the lives of all those involved in it, students and educators alike.

Dr. Louis Finkelstein, a former chancellor of the Jewish Theological Seminary of America, once said that when he prayed, he talked to God. But when he studied (Jewish texts), God talked to him! Jewish education is no less than a dialogue with God, in which case, all Jews share the responsibility, as individuals and a community, for improving their communications skills. Therefore, may the entire Jewish community strive to become better partners in this eternal, ongoing conversation with God via Jewish education.

Glossary

A Fortiori—Latin; an argument based on an inference. In Hebrew, a *Kal v'Homer* argument where two cases are compared, one lenient, one strict. If the law is strict in a serious case, how much more so will the law be strict when applied to the lenient case.

Aggadah (adjective: *Aggadic*)—All Rabbinic literature that has nothing to do with Jewish law (*Halakhah*). Aggadic literature is characterized by stories, fables, and sayings.

Aliyot—Literally, "to go up." Refers to a synagogue honor where a congregant is called up to recite a blessing over the reading of the Torah.

Amidah—Literally, "standing." Refers to central prayer that is at the core of each of the three daily prayer services in the Jewish tradition.

Amoraim—The title of the Rabbis who created the *Gemara*, a comprehensive discussion and analysis of the *Mishnah*. These Rabbis lived in Israel and Babylonia and were active during the years 220 to 500 C.E.

Arba'ah Turim—Literally, "The Four Columns." A medieval Jewish legal code written by Rabbi Ya'acov ben Asher in 1475.

Ashrei—Literally, "Happy are they." A verse from Psalms 84:5, which serves as an introduction to Psalm 145. This is a central prayer recited in the morning and afternoon services in the Jewish tradition.

Av—The Hebrew name of a summer month. On the ninth day of Av in the year 586 B.C.E., the First Temple was destroyed by the Babylonians and on the same day in 70 C.E., the Second Temple was destroyed by the Romans.

Avot D'Rabbi Natan—The name of a Rabbinic Midrashic commentary on Pirkei Avot, a tractate from the *Mishnah.*

Beit Midrash—"House of Study." In Jewish institutions, it refers to either a place of worship or study.

Bekiut—Literally, "expertise" or detailed knowledge of a subject.

Birkat HaMazon—"Blessing after meals." Recited after a meal where bread has been eaten.

Birkot HaShahar—"Blessings of the dawn." A series of introductory prayers and psalms recited each morning before the main core of the morning service, *Shaharit.*

Converso—Spanish for "convert." Used to refer to those Jews in Spain who chose to undergo conversion to Catholicism rather than face exile from their homes. Some of these converted Jews continued to practice Judaism in secret at the time of the Inquisition.

Daven—Yiddish for "pray." Often used to refer to the act of praying (*davening*).

Derekh Eretz—"The way of the land." Refers to the Jewish understanding of appropriate, polite behavior among people.

Drash—Literally, "to expound, explain, interpret." Usually refers to an imaginative explanation of a verse or passage from the Bible. The opposite of *peshat.*

D'var Torah (plural: *Divrei Torah*)—"Words of Torah." Refers to a short, sermonic or explanatory talk on the weekly Torah portion.

Etrog—A citrus fruit used for ritual purposes in the synagogue on the festival of Sukkot.

Gabbaim—Literally, "Money raisers." Traditionally refers to the honorific roles assigned to members of a congregation to assist in the service of reading from the Torah.

Gan Eden—The Garden of Eden.

Gehinom—The Rabbinic term used to refer to a place of spiritual torment for souls after death. The Jewish equivalent of Hell or Limbo. Considered only a temporary abode for wicked souls.

Gemara—Aramaic term meaning, "learning." Refers to the Rabbinic commentary, exposition, and analysis of the *Mishnah* by the *Amoraim* who lived in Israel and Babylonia from 220 to 500 C.E. Often used as a synonym for the Talmud. Therefore, there are two Gemaras, a Palestinian Talmud and a Babylonian Talmud.

Geniza—Literally, "To hide." Refers to a storage place where holy Jewish texts, such as Torah scrolls, prayer books, and printed Hebrew Bibles, are placed when they become too old or frayed to be used. Instead of being thrown out, they are stored until they can be buried, considered a more dignified disposal of holy texts.

G'lilah—Literally, "rolling." Refers to the honorific role a member of a congregation receives to assist in rolling up and covering a Torah scroll that has just been read. This role is fulfilled in conjunction with *Hagbah*.

Haftorah—A selection from the Prophets in the Bible, which is chanted on Shabbat and holidays after the Torah reading.

Hagbah—Literally, "lifting." Refers to the honorific role a member of a congregation receives to assist in lifting up a Torah scroll that has just been read. This role is fulfilled in conjunction with *G'lilah*.

Halakhah (Adjective: *Halakhic*)—Literally, "going" or "walking." Refers to all of Jewish ritual, religious, civil, and even criminal law from the Bible until modern times.

Hasidim—Literally, "the pious." Refers to ultra-Orthodox Jews who scrupulously observe the details of Jewish ritual laws. The Hasidic movement began in Poland in the late 1600's.

Haskalah—The Jewish "enlightenment" when European Jews enthusiastically embraced secular, non-Jewish learning in the 1800s.

Havruta—Aramaic for "partner" or "companion." Refers to pair or small group of students engaged in the cooperative study of traditional Jewish texts.

Hazzan—A Jewish cantor, or master of ritual synagogue music.

Hesed—Literally, "grace" or "graciousness." Also translated as "kindness."

Heshbon Nefesh—Literally, "taking account of the soul." An introspective, inward analysis that individual Jews are encouraged to do during the season of the High Holy Days in the Fall in order to facilitate *Teshuvah,* or repentance.

Kaddish—A prayer that appears in various permutations throughout the Jewish prayerbook, most commonly recited by mourners in a synagogue in memory of their departed family members.

Kadosh—Literally, "holy."

Kal V'Homer—Literally, "lenient and strict." See *A fortiori.*

Karaites—A fairly popular movement of Jews that flourished around 800 to 1000 c.e. These Jews rejected the Rabbinic tradition as recorded in the *Mishnah* and *Gemara* and asserted that only the Torah had religious validity. They were locked in constant debate with the Rabbinites, the adherents to the Rabbinic tradition.

Kashrut—The Jewish dietary laws.

Kavanah—Literally, "aim" or "focus." Refers to the kind of concentration and intensity of worship a Jew should strive to develop while engaged in prayer.

Ketuvim—Literally, "the Writings." This is the Hebrew term for the Hagiographia, the third section of the Hebrew

Bible, which contains such books as Psalms, Job, Proverbs, Song of Songs, Ruth, Lamentations, Eccelesiastes, and Esther.

Kohen (plural: *Kohanim*)—Literally, "priest." The subcaste of Israelites within the tribe of Levi who attended to the details of the sacrificial service when the ancient Temples stood in Jerusalem.

Ladino—A dialect of Spanish and Hebrew spoken by Jews of Spanish descent in Northern Africa, Italy, Greece, and Turkey.

Lulav—The palm branches used for ritual purposes in the synagogue on the festival of Sukkot.

Maariv—Literally, "evening." Refers to the evening prayer service in the Jewish tradition.

Malakhim—Literally, "messengers." Refers to angels in the Jewish tradition.

Mashiach—Literally, "annointed one." Refers to the Messiah, an individual appointed by God to restore all Jews to the land of Israel and establish universal peace.

Mechina—Literally, "preparation." Often used to refer to programs to help Jewish students increase their Jewish literacy and study skills in order to enter a mainstream program of Jewish studies.

Megillot—Literally, "scrolls." Refers to the five books in the Hebrew Bible (Song of Songs, Ruth, Lamentations, Eccelesiastes, and Esther), which are read at worship services for various holidays throughout the year.

Midah K'neged Midah—Literally, "measure for measure." A Rabbinic theological tenet holding that the way one sins determines the manner in which he or she will be punished.

Midrash (plural: *Midrashim*)—Literally, "an exposition, explanation." This is both a process and the results of this process. Usually refers to the Rabbis who interpreted the Bible and recorded their explanations.

Mikveh—A ritual bath for both Jewish men and women (separately) intended to spiritually purify the one who is immersed in it. The water must be from a natural source, such as rain.

Minha—The afternoon worship service in the Jewish tradition.

Minyon (plural: *Minyonim*)—Literally, "a counting." Refers to the minimum of ten adult Jews (traditionally males) required to worship as a community, that is, to say certain communal prayers. Also refers to any regular gathering of Jews to pray.

Mishmeret (plural: *Mishmarot*)—Literally, "a guarding period." When the Temple still stood, a *Mishmeret* consisted of a designated number of *Kohanim,* or priests, who would perform their appointed tasks in the Temple in Jerusalem in two-week "shifts." The *Kohanim* attended to the details of running an institution dedicated to animal sacrifices.

Mishnah (plural: *Mishnayot*)—The first Rabbinic codification of Jewish law, created and organized by the Tannaim from approximately after the destruction of the Second Temple in 70 C.E. and finally edited by Rabbi Yehudah HaNasi in 220 C.E. Next to the Torah, it is the most authoritative work on Jewish law. It consists of six Orders, or *Sedarim,* which contain numerous smaller tractates, or individual volumes on different topics.

Mishneh Torah—Literally, "the second Torah." The major code of Jewish law written by Rabbi Moses ben Maimon, also known as Maimonides (or his acronym, the Rambam), and published in 1177 in Egypt.

Mitnagdim—Literally, "the opposers." Refers to traditional Jews who opposed the establishment of the Hasidic movement in Poland in the 1600s.

Mitzvah (plural: *Mitzvot*)—Literally, "commandment." Often mistranslated as "good deed." *Mitzvah* refers to all activities that are understood to be commanded by God, including all ritual acts, such as praying, observing the Sabbath, and keeping *Kosher.* The *Mitzvot* also include ethical guidelines for people to live by, such as giving charity, honoring the elderly, and pursuing peace.

Musar—Literally, "ethics." Refers to a movement popular in Eastern European academies of traditional Jewish learning that emphasized appropriate ethical and moral conduct of its followers.

Neviim—Hebrew for "prophets." Refers to the second major section of the Hebrew Bible which contains the historical narratives of Joshua, Judges, Samuel, and Kings, as well as the prophetic books of Isaiah, Jeremiah, Ezekiel, and the twelve minor prophets.

Nikiyon—Literally, "cleanliness."

Olam HaBah—Literally, "the world to come." A Rabbinic concept used to refer to some form of continued spiritual existence for human beings after death.

Onesh—Literally, "punishment."

Peshat—Literally, "simple." It refers to the most simple, clearest, and contextual understanding of a text, usually the Bible. It is the plain meaning of a verse or passage. Opposite of *drash.*

Pesukei DeZimra—Literally, "verses of song." Refers to the introductory portion of morning worship services in the Jewish tradition. This section is composed of quotes from the book of Psalms and other portions throughout the Bible.

Pirkei Avot—Literally, "chapters of the fathers." The name of a tractate, or volume in the *Mishnah,* which in unique in that it contains no law, rather, only the ethical and moral statements and sayings of the *Tannaim,* the Rabbis who composed the *Mishnah.*

P'tihot—Literally, "openings." Refers to the honorific role assigned to members of a congregation to open and close the Ark in the Torah reading service.

Rabban—An ancient honorific title assigned to the leading Rabbi during the period of the *Mishnah,* approximately 70 C.E. to 220 C.E.

Rabbanites—Those Jews who maintained the divinity and authority of the Rabbis who interpreted the Bible for later generations of Jews. They were locked in constant debate with the Karaites, who asserted the authority of only the Bible to the exclusion of the *Mishnah* and *Gemara.*

Rabbis—The Rabbis (with a capital "R") refers to the original Jewish scholars and leaders who, following the destruction of the Second Temple in 70 C.E. by the Romans, transformed Judaism from a system dependent upon animal sacrifices into a comprehensive religion based on prayer. The Rabbis wrote the *Mishnah, Gemara* (together, known as the Talmud) as well as all of the *Midrashim.* All Jews today are Rabbinic Jews as a result of their efforts.

Rambam—An acronym and popular appellation for Rabbi Moses ben Maimon, also known as Maimonides. He wrote and published the *Mishneh Torah* in 1177 in Egypt.

Ramban—An acronym and popular appellation for Rabbi Moses ben Nachmun, also known as Nachmonides. He lived in Spain in the mid-1200s and wrote an influential mystical commentary on the Torah.

Rashi—An acronym and popular appellation for Rabbi Shlomo ben Yitzchak, who lived in Provence, France, in the mid-1000s and wrote what is considered to be the classic commentary on the Torah, blending *Peshat* and *Drash.*

Responsa—Rabbinic legal responses to legal questions. This is a form of legal literature that has served to expand and apply Jewish law throughout the ages.

Rosh HaShanah—Literally, "the new year." Usually this two-day holiday falls in September or early October. It marks the beginning of a new calendar year in the Jewish liturgical cycle. It is traditional for Jews to prepare for the High Holy Days by engaging in personal introspection and repentence for past misdeeds.

Rosh Hodesh—Literally, "the new moon." Because the Jewish calendar is based primarily on a lunar calendar, the appearance of the new moon, signaling the start of a new Hebrew month, is a minor holiday each month.

Sanhedrin—An ancient court of Rabbinical judges of civil and criminal cases that functioned in the land of Israel during the period of the Second Temple and the *Mishnah*. It is also the name of a tractate (volume) in the *Mishnah* that describes its function.

Seder (plural: *Sedarim*)—Literally, "order." It refers to one of the six major divisions of the *Mishnah*. The names of the six divisions indicate the major portion of their contents: Seeds (agricultural law), Festivals, Women (personal status laws), Damages (torts and criminal law), Holy things (referring to animal sacrifices), and Purities (referring to laws dealing with ritual purity and impurity). Because the word *seder* means order, it is also the name for the ritual Passover banquet in which Jews recount the story of the exodus from Egypt.

Shabbat—Literally, "rest." Saturday, the Jewish day of rest. Characterized by prayer, family meals, and relaxation. Despite the fact that it falls once a week, Shabbat is considered to be the holiest day of the entire calendar, surpassing even the Jewish High Holy Days.

Shaharit—Literally, "dawn." Refers to the morning prayer service held every day, whether weekday, Shabbat, or holiday.

Shavuot—Literally, "weeks." The pilgrimage festival, also known as Pentacost, that falls seven weeks after Passover. It commemorates the giving of the Torah on Mt. Sinai.

Shema—Literally, "Listen!" Refers to the central axiom of Jewish belief from Deuteronomy 4:6. This passage and other related texts from the Torah are recited each morning and evening in Jewish prayer.

Shulkhan Arukh—Literally, "a prepared table." This is the name of the classic compendium of Jewish law written by Joseph Karo and Moshe Isserles and published in 1567.

Siddur (plural: *Siddurim*)—Literally, "order." A generic term for any Jewish prayer book. The word *Siddur* is related to the Hebrew word *seder*, meaning order. Therefore, a *siddur* lays out the order of the prayers to be recited by a worshipper.

S'khar—Literally, "reward." In the world of Rabbinic literature, this is often used in the phrase, "*s'khar v'onesh*," meaning "reward and punishment," referring to Divine justice in worldly, human affairs.

Sukkot—Literally, "booths." The pilgrimage festival, also known as the Feast of Booths, which occurs in the Fall. It commemorates the journey of the Israelites through the desert for forty years.

Talit (plural: *Talitot*)—A Jewish prayer shawl with fringes (*tzitzit*) on each of the four corners.

Tanakh—An acronym in Hebrew comprised of the first three letters of the three sections of the Bible: *Torah, Neviim,* and *Ketuvim*. It refers to the Hebrew Bible.

Tannaim—Literally, "the repeaters." The title of the Rabbis who created the *Mishnah,* so-called because they committed their enormous store of learning to memory alone and recited their lessons and knowledge orally.

Tefillah (plural: *Tefillot*)—Jewish prayers.

Tefillin—A variant of the Hebrew word for prayer, this refers to phylacteries or small leather boxes containing sections of the Torah that are secured with leather straps to the head and arm of an adult Jew during the morning weekday prayer service.

Tehillim—The book of Psalms in the Bible.

Tehiyat HaMetim—Literally, "resurrection of the dead." A central belief of the Rabbis who created the Talmud and Midrashic works.

Teshuvah—Literally, "turning." It refers to the practice of repentence, that is, recognizing one's transgressions, regretting them, and ensuring that they will not be repeated. Encouraged during the High Holy Day season.

Tikkun Olam—Literally, "repairing the world." Refers to the Jewish mandate to work for social and economic justice in the world.

Torah—Literally, "instruction." The name of the Five Books of Moses, which contains the essential narrative and laws of the Jewish people.

Torah Trope—The musical cantillation or notes by which the Torah portion of the week is chanted in synagogue.

Tractate—A volume of both *Mishnah* and *Gemara,* the Talmud.

Tzedakah—Literally, "justice." The commandment that Jews must work for social and economic equity in society.

Tzitzit—The fringes that adorn the four corners of a *talit,* a Jewish prayer shawl.

Yetzer HaRah—Literally, "the evil inclination." In Rabbinic theology, it is the primal urge in all human beings that leads us not only to transgress the bounds of appropriate behavior, but to earn a living, seek a mate, and raise a family.

Yetzer HaTov—Literally, "the good inclination." In Rabbinic theology, it is the desire to act appropriately and do good.

Yigdal—Literally, "He will be magnified" referring to God. This is the first word and name of a synagogue hymn whose words are based on the thirteen basic Jewish beliefs as imagined by Maimonides, although not universally accepted.

Yom Kippur—Literally, "the day of atonement." Next to Shabbat, which falls once a week, Yom Kippur is the holiest day of the Jewish calendar, a day set aside for fasting and prayer.

Zohar—Literally, "light." The name of the classic medieval book of Jewish mysticism.

Select Bibliography
of
Recommended Sources

Bible Studies

Chumash and Rashi, Translated into English and annotated by Rabbi A. M. Silberman, published by Feldheim Publishers (Jerusalem, 1934). A five-volume translation of Rashi's classic commentary on the Talmud with helpful endnotes.

JPS Tanakh and Commentary, published by the Jewish Publication Society in five volumes (Philadelphia, 1994). An important and useful commentary on the Torah filled with insights from traditional Rabbinic commentaries as well as modern archeology and anthropology. The excursus at the end of each volume are invaluable.

The Tanakh, published by the Jewish Publication Society (Philadelphia, 1988). The most up-to-date, accurate, scholarly translation of the Hebrew Bible.

Teaching Torah: A Treasury of Insights and Activities, by Sorel Goldberg Loeb and Barbara Binder Kadden, published by Alternatives in Religious Education, Inc. (Denver, 1984). A summary of each weekly Torah portion along with selections of Rabbinic texts and suggested activities for children of all ages as well as adults.

Exploring Exodus, by Nahum Sarna, published by Schocken Books (New York, 1986). A continuation of the literary and anthropological analysis of the Torah, focusing on the book of Exodus.

Understanding Genesis, by Nahum Sarna, published by Schocken Books (New York, 1966). A concise literary and anthropological analysis of the book of Genesis filled with parallels to other ancient cultures in the Middle East.

Rabbinics

Aiding Talmud Study, by Aryeh Carmell, published by Feldheim Publishers (Jerusalem, 1980). A brief book that includes a short dictionary of common Aramaic phrases and concepts, charts with Talmudic measurements and coinage mentioned in the Talmud, and other diagrams for quick reference while studying Talmud.

A Dictionary of the Targumim, Talmud Babli, Yerushalmi, and Midrashic Literature, compiled by Marcus Jastrow, published by Judaica Press, Inc. (New York, 1982). The classic dictionary essential for all text study of the *Mishnah, Gemara,* and Midrashic works.

The Essential Talmud, by Adin Steinsaltz, published by Basic Books. An excellent introduction to the history, contents, and philosophy of the Rabbis who created the *Gemara.*

Everyman's Talmud, by Abraham Cohen, published by Schocken Books (New York, 1975). A summary and anthology of relevant Rabbinic texts from the Talmud on the theology of human life, God, revelation, and divine justice, as well as practical issues outlining the Jewish legal system and determining what constitutes the "good" life. The first book to consult when researching any topic in the Talmud.

Introduction to the Talmud, by Moses Mielziner, published by Bloch Publishing Co. (New York, 1968). A classic 75-year-old introduction to Talmudic hermeneutics and methodology, filled with references and examples.

The Midrash Rabbah, published by Soncino Press (London, 1983). A ten-volume translation (with an index) of the major Midrashic works on the books of the Bible.

Mishnayot, translated by Philip Blackman, published by Judaica Press (New York, 1963). An English translation of the *Mishnah* with explanations and footnotes in seven volumes (with an index).

A Rabbinic Anthology, by C. G. Montefiore and H. Loewe, published by Schocken Books (New York, 1974). An older version of *Everyman's Talmud,* which provides a similar anthology of Rabbinic quotes on a wide spectrum of theological topics.

The Soncino Talmud, published by Soncino Press (London, 1935). An eighteen-volume translation of the Talmud (with an index).

The Talmud, The Steinsaltz Edition: A Reference Guide, by Adin Steinsaltz, published by Random House (New York, 1976). A treasury of technical information about the history, language, vocabulary, and legal concepts employed by the Rabbis in the *Mishnah* and *Gemara.* A must for actual Talmudic text study.

Understanding the Talmud, by R. Yitzchak Feigenbaum, published by Darche Noam Publications. A clear, easy-to-follow dictionary of common technical Aramaic phrases and concepts employed in the Talmud. A must for actual Talmudic text study.

Jewish History

A History of Israel, by John Bright, published by Westminster Press (Philadelphia, 1981). A scholarly presentation of the historical origins of the Israelites, covering the Biblical period.

A History of Israel, by Howard Sacher, published by Knopf (New York, 1982). The best one-volume work available about the origins of Zionism and the creation of the state of the Israel up until relatively modern times.

A History of the Jewish People, edited by H. H. Ben-Sasson, published by Harvard University Press (Cambridge, MA, 1976). A scholarly one-volume presentation of the history of the Jewish people from Biblical times to the modern state of Israel. Each section is written by a scholar in the particular field at Hebrew University in Jerusalem. Not an easy read.

A History of the Jews, by Cecil Roth, published by Schocken (New York, 1970). A light, but thorough presentation of the history of the Jewish people from Biblical times to the founding of the state of Israel.

Hebrew Language

The Complete Hebrew–English Dictionary, by Reuben Alcalay, published by Massada Publishing Co. (Jerusalem, 1981). A three-volume, comprehensive Hebrew–English and English–Hebrew dictionary.

Ha-Yesod: Fundamentals of Hebrew, by Luba Uveeler and Norman M. Bronznick, published by Feldheim Publishers (Jerusalem, 1980). A thorough introduction to the Hebrew language, for adults and teenagers. Covers all aspects of grammer and builds a solid vocabulary.

Hebrew: The Eternal Language, by William Chomsky, published by the Jewish Publication Society (Philadelphic, 1957). A history of the Hebrew language from its ancient semitic roots to its rebirth as a modern, spoken language in Israel.

Jewish Philosophy/Theology

Finding God: Ten Jewish Responses, by Rifat Sonsino and Daniel B. Syme, published by the Union of American Hebrew Congregations (New York, 1986). A summary of ten different classic Jewish understandings of God. Intended as a resource for teachers.

Jewish People, Jewish Thought, by Robert Seltzer, published by Macmillan Press (New York, 1980). A scholarly intellectual history of the Jewish people from its origins to modern times. An excellent reference for historical events as well as for philosophy and theology.

The Judaic Tradition, edited by Nahum Glatzer, published by Beacon Press (Boston, 1969). A classic anthology of original passages and selections about Jewish philosophy and theology from the Bible up to modern times.

Knowing God, by Elliot Dorff, published by Aronson Press (Northvale, NJ). A readable, comprehensive introduction to modern Jewish philosophy.

Three Jewish Philosophers: Philo, Saadya Gaon, Jehudah Halevy, published by Atheneum Press (New York, 1969). Lengthy excerpts from the writings of three of the most articulate and influential classical Jewish philosophers.

Literary Genres

The Aggadic Midrash Literature, by Hananel Mack, published by MOD Books (Tel Aviv, 1989). A scholarly presentation of the various genres of *Midrash.*

The Art of Biblical Narrative and *The Art of Biblical Poetry,* by Robert Alter, published by Basic Books (New York, 1981 & 1985). Two thorough, insightful, and eye-opening books explaining and clarifying the underlying features and styles of the two major formats of Biblical literature.

Back to the Sources, edited by Barry W. Holtz, published by Summit Books (New York, 1984). An anthology of articles by leading scholars explaining the essence of Biblical, Rabbinic, Midrashic, and Kabbalistic texts.

An Introduction to Old Testament Study, by John H. Hayes, published by Abingdon Press (Nashville, 1979). A thorough historical presentation of the growing field of literary analysis of the Bible.

Invitation to Talmud and *Invitation to Midrash,* by Jacob Neusner, published by Harper & Row (San Francisco, 1984 & 1989). Excellent introductions to and analysis of textual examples of *Gemara* and different kinds of *Midrash.*

The Literary Guide to the Bible, edited by Robert Alter and Frank
Kermode, published by Belknap Press of Harvard University
Press (Cambridge, MA, 1987). An anthology of articles by top
Biblical scholars analyzing every book in the Hebrew Bible.

Reading the Book: Making the Bible a Timeless Text, by Burton L. Visot-
zky, published by Anchor Books (New York, 1991). A popular,
light exposition of how the Rabbis engaged in the process of
making *Midrash* on the Bible.

Prayer and Jewish Practice

To Be a Jew, by Hayim Halevy Donin, published by Basic Books (New
York, 1972). A concise introduction to the major elements of
Jewish ritual life from a traditional point of view.

A Guide to Jewish Religious Practice, by Isaac Klein, published by the
Jewish Theological Seminary (New York, 1979). A comprehensive explanation of all relevant aspects of modern Jewish ritual
practice from a traditional point of view in the Conservative
Movement.

Jewish Holidays: A Guide and Commentary, by Michael Strassfeld, published by Harper & Row (New York, 1985). Explains in detail the
customs and meanings of all Jewish holidays. The essays exploring the deeper theological and spiritual aspects of the holidays
are especially moving.

Jewish Worship, by Abraham Milgram, published by the Jewish
Publication Society (Philadelphia, 1971). A thorough, precise
presentation of all Jewish prayers and holiday liturgy with
explanations.

To Pray as a Jew, by Hayim Halevy Donin, published by Basic Books
(New York, 1980). An excellent introduction to daily and
Shabbat prayers, complete with translations, explanations, and
diagrams to illustrate the choreography of the movements of
Jewish prayer.

General

Basic Judaism, by Rabbi Milton Steinberg, published by Harcourt,
Brace, Jovanovich. A lucid presentation of the Jewish religion in
very broad, general terms.

Emotional Intelligence, by Daniel Goleman, published by Bantam
Books (New York, 1995). Explores the skills that make for successful teachers and students in the classroom, and people in
their everyday lives.

Encyclopedia Judaica, by Keter Publishing (Jerusalem, 1973). The classic seventeen-volume exploration of everything Jewish. Covers an enormous range of topics on Judaism and Jewish history, with detailed access via an index volume.

Jewish Literacy, by Joseph Telushkin, published by William Morrow and Co. (New York, 1991). Subtitled "The Most Important Things to Know about the Jewish Religion, Its People, and Its History," it keeps its promise and provides references for further study.

Leadership for the Schoolhouse, by Thomas J. Sergiovanni, published by Jossey-Bass Publishers (San Francisco, 1996). An enlightening book intended for principals and administrators in public schools that unintentionally explores the advantages of Jewish education.

Managing the Jewish Classroom: How to Transform Yourself into a Master Teacher, by Seymour Rossel, published by Torah Aura Productions (Los Angeles, 1987). A very good "how-to" book on teaching primarily elementary school children, complete with suggestions of classroom activities.

The Nine Questions People Ask About Judaism, by Dennis Prager and Joseph Telushkin, published by Simon and Schuster (New York, 1981). A very provocative, partisan book about basic Jewish beliefs. The strongly stated viewpoints of the authors leave little or no room for alternative rationales for the Jewish tradition. Good fodder for more sophisticated analysis of Judaism.

Index

About the Author

DANIEL B. KOHN is Associate Rabbi and educator at Congregation Kol Shofar in Tiburon, California.